Boosting boys' motivation in MFL

Boosting boys' motivation in MFL

Also available from CILT, the National Centre for Languages

Boys' performance in Modern Foreign Languages: Listening to learners
Barry Jones and Gwenneth Jones et al

It makes you think!: Creating engagement, offering challenges
(New Pathfinder 4)
Barry Jones and Ann Swarbrick

The Centre for Information on Language Teaching and Research provides a complete range of services for language professionals in every stage and sector of education, and in business, in support of its brief to promote Britain's foreign language capability.

CILT is a registered charity, supported by Central Government grants. CILT is based in Covent Garden, London, and its services are delivered through a national collaborative network of regional Comenius Centres in England, CILT Cymru, Northern Ireland CILT and Scottish CILT.

Boosting boys' motivation in MFL

Barry Jones

with 'A focus on homework' by Moira Edmunds

Acknowledgements

In some cases (pp13–21) it has not been possible to trace copyright holders of material reproduced in this book. The publisher will be pleased to make the appropriate arrangement at the earliest opportunity with any copyright holder whom it has not been possible to contact.

First published 2005 by CILT, the National Centre for Languages, 20 Bedfordbury, London WC2N 4LB

Copyright © CILT, the National Centre for Languages 2005

Cover photography © Robert Davies

ISBN 1 904243 38 X

A catalogue record for this book is available from the British Library

Printed by Hobbs the Printers, Totton, Hampshire

CILT Publications are available from: Central Books, 99 Wallis Rd, London E9 5LN. Tel: 0845 458 9910. Fax: 0845 458 9912.

Contents

Introduction

Much has been said and written about boys' (under-)performance in Modern Foreign Languages (MFL) in UK secondary schools. A study *Boys' performance in MFL: Listening to learners* (Jones and Jones 2001) commissioned by the Qualifications and Curriculum Authority (QCA), and published in 2001 by CILT, has 47 references to books, journal and press articles and official reports containing comment on, and often a detailed study of this phenomenon. This 2001 publication offers, as the title suggests, further insights by emphasising a pupil perspective in the data gathering and by highlighting the usefulness of listening to what boys – and some girls – have to say about MFL teaching and learning. Its final chapter contains a summary of twelve key findings and makes thirteen recommendations for practice and policy.

Since 2001 these recommendations have been the springboard for school-based action designed to enhance the performance of boys learning a foreign language in secondary school. For the last four years it has been my privilege to work with more than a hundred teachers in different parts of England and Wales and to co-ordinate their imaginative and creative attempts to put the recommendations into practice. What these teachers have done either on their own or working with others is what this book describes. Without their enthusiasm and sense of fun, always in evidence at the many meetings held during this time, my job would have been impossible. It is to them that this book is dedicated.

Regional projects

From 2001 there have been eight active groups of teachers in different parts of the country. They are geographically widespread and were formed, in all cases, as an outcome of an in-service event held within their local area. Each participant came to an introductory presentation, with a focus on the key findings and recommendations contained within the CILT publication, *Boys' performance in MFL*. As one of the report's co-authors I was able to illustrate and discuss during these initial meetings what boys had told us about their MFL lessons, what they thought worked well, what they found less engaging and what they – and their teachers – might do to help their learning improve. They were often perceptive and in interviews, forthcoming, realistic, and thoughtful. They frequently saw that their teacher's job was not easy!

In order to attempt to enhance boys' performance in MFL lessons in their own schools, participating teachers decided, mostly as the concluding activity in their initial in-service session, on a particular focus, often involving one or two year specific groups, which they proposed to develop once back in school. Some teachers decided on a joint venture and planned to work collaboratively with one or more neighbouring schools. Others decided to work alone or with other members of the MFL department in their own school. A small number of schools had a whole-school policy already in place, designed to address boys' performance in a number of curricular areas. In this situation the MFL teachers felt better able to contribute to an ongoing enterprise. Two teachers had received a Best Practice

Research Scholarship and one had a clear brief to investigate 'whether the implementation of the key findings and recommendations (in *Boys' performance in MFL*) could enhance the learning of pupils initially at Key Stage 3 (KS3) and longer term at Key Stage 4 (KS4)'.

The nature of the projects

The school-based activities were designed to enhance boys' performance in MFL. In nearly all participating schools boys and girls were involved although many of the projects and activities were ones which boys identified as ones which did or would potentially appeal to them. The number (in brackets) indicates the number of schools/groups who were engaged in a similar or identical project, but who were not necessarily working together.

All had as their objective to explore aspects of the recommendations in the CILT publication. Each recommendation here is followed by indications of teachers' agreed areas for experimentation and projects within their schools . Every ongoing project or activity started is mentioned and described. Evaluation of the positive effects of the projects is based on teacher testimony – what seemed to make a difference, where there were changes in pupil attitude, greater feelings of confidence, improved grades. Although some might claim that this is subjective the teachers involved were almost all very experienced and their testimony counts. If a project was not successful this is also reported.

RECOMMENDATIONS FOR PRACTICE AND FOR POLICY

The recommendations relate to points (shown in bold) made in the 'Summary of key findings and recommendations for practice and policy' (see Boys' performance in MFL, *Jones and Jones 2001: 46–49); numbers refer to what boys said and the letter T to teachers' comments. They are formulated partly as a response to problems which boys identified in the study but had no answers for, and partly to reflect some of the boys' positive suggestions and experiences.*

Part 1

Helping boys improve:
School-based projects

1

Focus on what we teach and real uses for the Modern Foreign Language

1 Content for MFL

Create opportunities for learners to speak to native speakers – student teachers, a Foreign Language Assistant (FLA), other adults, other children – either face-to-face or via e-mail, fax, or from a website. This may illustrate the 'reality factor' for learners, especially boys.
1a 1g 3 6 11

Ensuring an audience: communicating with a purpose

Fifteen projects were based on the first recommendation. These were:

1   A teacher, working on his own, devised a programme for a bottom set Year 10 group, mostly boys, to teach basic German in a local primary school. This included teaching numbers 1–20 and doing mathematical sums with them, then teaching the alphabet and developing accurate spelling. There was initially a half hour lesson each week. Although this initiative very successfully encouraged the Year 10 boys to improve their own linguistic competence – and to make their own materials – in order to teach the foreign language accurately to the younger children the project stalled for a while until the teacher in charge from the secondary school had gained a First Aid Certificate, a requirement of the LEA for those working in a primary school!

2   Two schools had a Year 10 group devise a quiz in French and fax it to other schools in the UK. This was also done by a third school with pupils in another country – Bulgaria – where the sole lingua franca was the target language (French). A fourth school established a quiz link with Germany with questions in the target language. The quizzes, in most cases, were theme-based and related to topics required in the GCSE examination, although in one case it focused on general subject knowledge. In other schools teachers and pupils explored developing quizzes by older learners for lower ability or younger groups within the same school.

3   Several projects encouraged boys and girls to use the MFL for a genuine purpose and with a specific and real audience. These activities included making a video, taking part in a Language Day, running an inter-class song writing competition, setting up an imaginary estate agent to 'sell' their own houses, putting on a 'outlandish outfit' fashion show for parents in the summer term with French food and drink made and served by pupils. Other projects involved role play and drama productions, devised with the explicit intention of demonstrating, in the words of one boy, that 'MFL learning is not just an academic pursuit'. In one instance the MFL and a drama teacher helped a Year 10 group produce advertisements which were subsequently displayed at a parents' evening. There were also activities which involved making presentations to the rest of the class – and to other classes – to recap vocabulary, show language in context, explain grammar in their own words, and to revise a topic. Boys also enjoyed teaching parts of a lesson, producing

their own materials and resources (overhead projector transparencies, clip art pictures and flashcards, board games …, developing and running an activity within a lesson with the teacher sitting in the wings while they ran a game, a competition or a quiz, and working on collaborative project such as producing a tourists' guide to a town, or writing briefing notes for the new Foreign Language Assistant. An imaginative project which appealed especially to boys was called 'How well do you know the Foreign Language *Assistante*?' In this example the boys, as well as girls, had to ask questions, then remember – and record – the replies they received. They then passed on the information to the teacher either orally or in writing depending on their ability and the 'best reporter' was rewarded with *bons points*. In Wales this was made into an interschool competition which took place early on in the year when the *Assistantes* had just arrived.

4   A number of schools (seven) established e-mail links with other schools within the Francophone world, Guadeloupe, Martinique and Canada. One group of Year 8 pupils sent e-mails to a school in Germany via **www.epals.com** and other links were established with schools in Spain.

Here is one teacher's evaluation of using e-mail.

E-mail link

Advantages

- **Raised the awareness of the foreign language, culture and customs.**

- **Contact and friendships with foreign students, creating a genuine reason for learning the language.**

- **Reduced phobia and ignorance of life abroad.**

- **Opportunity to pick up every day language use and slang that they love using in class.**

Disadvantages

- **Time consuming setting up the link.**

- **Computer access is limited due to timetables and pupils are reluctant to give up their breaks and lunch times.**

- **When computers crash due to a virus, letters take a long time to be written and sent. Loss of motivation!**

Source: Chris Williams, St Thomas More RC High School, North Shields

---

5   In one instance pupils' written work was used as a resource and revision for other learners and to give the originators a genuine readership. Communication with other pupils was by work displayed on school notice boards. Two other projects exchanged e-mail messages within and between schools, and developed further communication by fax.

6   Some teachers devised a systematic programme in school to promote MFL through real-life situations such as talking to people using the internet, viewing films and videos (*Taxi 1, Taxi 2, Amélie, Le café des rêves, Hennings Haus, Top* (the Channel 4 gameshow) making personal contacts, visiting the website **www.epals.com**. As an activity to be presented at the European Day of Languages a Head of Department in a mixed comprehensive school produced a video where every child in the school, from Year 7 to the Sixth form, said at least one thing in a foreign language to the camera. This involved more than a thousand pupils. The recording was used at appropriate moments during lessons and over time, always with the participants' permission, to demonstrate progress, to encourage class comment which had to be positive, and to show others what individual pupils could do.

7   A growing number of teachers set up and encouraged PowerPoint presentations, often but not exclusively by Year 10 and 11 students, with a MFL teaching staff check, designed to help their peers and/or younger MFL learners in school.

Content included:

- *Ma maison* presented by Year 11 for Year 7 learners. The presentation was also used as a resource in a homework club.

- Spreadsheets produced by Year 11 working in pairs, collating information about each person in a group, describing what they liked doing, what type of TV programmes they watched, where they worked part-time. If this is in the form 'I work in a hairdressers' shop and I ...' and if a number of pupils produce descriptions along these lines others can try to guess who the writers are, either as a class competition or as work on the classroom walls, for those who finish early to read and identify.

Year 10 pupils were also involved, one group developing teaching materials on colours for Year 7. The pupils who demonstrated their PowerPoint resource were very nervous as they did so, but proud of their achievement afterwards.

Boys in particular responded positively to this initiative. This was illustrated in one school when the teacher said to a class that she did not know how to use PowerPoint so allowed a boy to take over the technical side while she provided the language. Other Year 10 boys taught a ten minute slot to Year 7 again using PowerPoint. The teacher emphasised that the language had been agreed and checked before the older pupils started work. A third Year 10 class, mainly boys, also produced presentations for younger and lower ability groups, but made copies available for all the teachers in the MFL department to use. Two boys and two girls in another Year 10, working together, illustrated all the uses of *avoir* in French for Year 9 learners. Throughout the project, they were in charge and produced a five minute presentation during which they were responsible for answering all the questions from the class. Another interesting example was a mixed ability, Year 10 group who taught each other using PowerPoint how to form the present tense of *-er*, *-ir*, and *-re* verbs in French. The teacher reported that the girls worked together as a group but the boys preferred to work on their own, showing perhaps that choice of working groupings, and different ways of working, may be a factor in engaging boys. This could usefully be explored further.

8   Two Specialist Language Colleges, with videoconferencing facilities, involved different groups of learners in each college. Each school had pupils talk to each other on well-rehearsed topics.

9   Two schools provided a collection of teenage magazines, chosen and bought by, in one instance, Year 11 pupils and in another, by pupils of different ages, during school visits to France. A small group of pupils, sensitively selected, was given a budget in euros equivalent to £60. Each spent a morning in a French *librairie* selecting magazines which they felt would interest other pupils, both boys and girls, of the same or similar ages. Their choice was popular in school and included themes such as fishing, mountain biking, surfing, animals, cycling, football, motorbikes, skate boarding, teenage fashion, lifestyle and preoccupations. Only one publication with cartoons was included because most pupils felt these were too difficult to understand. Both schools had a system for readers to note the name of the publication and the title (or page) of the article, to give the publication a rating and to select an adjective or a sentence to summarise their reactions to the chosen text. Formats for these evaluations were taken from Ann Swarbrick's two excellent publications *Reading for pleasure in a foreign language* (1990) and its sequel *More reading for pleasure in a foreign language* (1998) both published by CILT.

10 One school set up an in-school Bulletin Board in German for pupil-to-pupil talk. This was updated regularly and boys and girls seemed interested in not only reading what others had written but also in seeing their own messages, comments, advertisements, cartoons, etc on display.

11 Several teachers experimented with a range of creative activities such as storytelling, writing poems, fictional/imaginary descriptions, fake messages, raps, as well as including mime, movement and performance in their lessons. Personal use of the target language, as well as physical activity did appear to engage boys as well as girls in using the language they were learning. Boys particularly appreciated having a model for what they wrote, especially writing frames which provided a clear structure. They liked end products which showed their photo taken with a digital camera.

12 Activities which promoted 'thinking skills' were popular since boys, as well as girls, seemed to like solving puzzles. Examples of these can be found in Barry Jones and Ann Swarbrick's New Pathfinder 4: *It makes you think!* (CILT 2004). These were especially popular with boys when there was a time limit – for example how many sentences/words/phrases on the theme of … can you produce in three minutes? Or how long can you make a description about … in two minutes? This works particularly well if made into an inter-class competition, involving two similar year groups. Competition is thus either against the class's own best result or that of another class.

13 One school had Year 12 male students (not necessarily MFL specialists) working with younger MFL classes as part of the school's community service activities. This was particularly effective from the teachers' perspective when it was the Year 12 student who set the homework tasks. Not only were these better done but also more regularly handed in when the work went to the student than when the teacher was involved!

14 For a Year 8 class motivation was increased when the teacher, tackling the topic of food and drink in Spanish, suggested that all the pupils should look through the shelves in their large, high street supermarket and try to spot what came from Spain. This activity was done by both boys and girls with great enthusiasm.

15 Collaborative work especially with pupils working in pairs (for example deciding on an answer together before being asked to provide a response during question and answer work) seemed to take the pressure off boys – and girls, too – and to give them a chance to come up with a response without losing face or feeling threatened in front of their peers. Pairwork which included an emotional content, or 'attitude' was seen as more engaging than playing the parts 'straight'. To encourage this dramatic version 'emotions' are written onto individual visiting cards and given out at random to each child after they have rehearsed the role play in a standard way; it is important the players rehearse the language thoroughly first otherwise 'being dramatic' does not work so well. The list of emotions included the following:

furieux	**impatient**
furieuse	**impatiente**
paresseux	content
paresseuse	contente
de bonne humeur	***pressé***
	pressée
inquiet	
inquiète	**de mauvaise humeur**
gentil	poli
gentille	polie
impoli	*malheureux*
impolie	*malheureuse*
triste	

wütend	ungeduldig
faul	**zufrieden**
gut gelaunt	gestresst
beunruhigt	**unfreundlich**
nett	**höflich**
unhöflich	unglücklich
traurig	

16 Perhaps surprisingly only two MFL departments planned lessons to incorporate more strategies and content designed specifically to motivate boys, with an emphasis, in one case, on sporting personalities and sporting and business terminology, and in another on regularly creating time in each lesson for boys to move about and do something physical. The first initiative was justified by the teachers as a counterbalance to the content of course books which, they believed, emphasised the interpersonal, the family, and self presentation which boys were less inclined to engage with than girls. Boys in this school when asked about their MFL lessons were particularly forthcoming about their lack of interest in using and developing transactional language and were very enthusiastic when factual texts, business language and business contexts were included. They also appreciated their teacher's efforts to make textbook or GCSE themes and topics relevant to them, for example, why their own town was 'boring' or 'good' in terms of entertainment, what their preferences were, etc. Towns abroad had limited appeal but this could be increased if comparisons could be made between a home town and one in the target language country, especially if the school already had established links which could result in a visit.

Initiatives such as these clearly reflect one of the main findings in *Boys' performance in MFL*, namely:

> *[These activities and approaches] may also decrease the centrality of the teacher in the learning process, provide engaging content some of which can be chosen by the learner, emphasise content as well as language, show the relevance of MFL when communicating fact and information, and link language skills more coherently.* **1a 1c 1d 1g 1h 1I**

Exploring the use of the target language: links to the National Language Strategy

A related subset of the first recommendation in the report was to:

> *Encourage an exploration of the target language as both the medium and the object of study. The National Literacy Strategy (NLS) may have launched aspects which younger learners and their teachers can build on immediately.* **1b 1d 1g**

There were six projects based on this recommendation.

1 One school took advantage of strategies practised and used in earlier work in the school based on the National Literacy Strategy. This project had the particular aim of exploring sound-writing relationships, looking for patterns and improving spelling, the last being reported as problematic particularly for boys. It also aimed to develop reading strategies such as skimming and scanning, and in oral and written work, to encourage learners to give reasons and opinions for statements they made. In some schools the use of 'connectives' (*et, puis, alors, mais, par contre,* etc) was seen as an efficient and relatively straightforward way of extending the length and complexity of pupils' utterances. Since these were on permanent display in the classroom it became a game and a challenge, especially appreciated by the boys, to include as many of these words as possible in reply to the teacher's questions. This work on connectives and extending language utterances was taken up by several schools, both Middle and Secondary. One used a points' system for the choice of connective successfully used:

These were listed in the classroom and answers which included any were awarded the number of points shown below:

et	**1**
mais	**2**
puis	**3**
si	**4**
donc	**4**
alors	**4**
cependant	**5**

Another focused on getting their classes to extend the language used in oral responses by the inclusion of reasons for what was said. Again *bons points* were awarded for the use of:

parce que	**4**
à mon avis	**4**
je l'ai trouvé	**5**

To complete the reason given, learners could use a word from a list of adjectives on display:

affreux	*fantastique*
bizarre	*formidable*
chouette	*génial*
cool	*nul*
ennuyeux	*extra*

If further adverbs and qualifiers were included the greater the credit!

These included the following and were permanently on display for any group to use.

absolument

très

trop

vraiment

peut-être

un peu

2   A second school, which already had a policy of teaching Geography – one lesson weekly – through the medium of French tried to discover whether boys in particular, as well as girls, were motivated by the project. In the scheme of work the topic of *Settlement* was chosen since *Settlement* was usually covered in Geography lessons in Year 7 so key concepts were familiar and learning and discussion in the target language, therefore, less of a problem. The topic also involved the use of known vocabulary in the target language e.g. in French *une ville moyenne, un appartement, une maison moyenne, la banlieue*, etc. Cultural awareness was also developed which appealed to both boys and girls, but, in the boys' evaluation, was especially appreciated.

3   The target language was used for instructions for constructing and/or making things such as origami, toys, a fortune teller, puppets, as well as for more ambitious projects

such as cooking (*gazpacho, mousse au chocolat* …), making *Karneval* masks, putting on a fashion show …

4   The target language was, on occasion, used by the MFL teacher, to teach other curriculum areas for a lesson or a short period of time. PE, games, fitness instruction and cookery were the themes of these lessons when they occurred.

5   Work with other departments seemed to engage boys especially when cross-curricular themes were developed. Examples included: work with a drama department producing 'scenes from everyday life' (one school), the pantomime, *Aschenputtel* – Cinderella – (another school) and advertisements for a parents' evening (third school); with a food technology department (Year 8) developing the theme of food in another country, with recipes, instructions, equipment; with a music and dance teacher producing dance routines for a musical.

6   A Year 8 teacher made explicit links with her Geography, History and other French colleagues to teach collaboratively about St Lucia, Martinique and Guadeloupe – St Lucia was being taught in Geography at the same time. Topics included the slave trade, growing bananas, music festivals, motorbike racing, and a 'hurricane drill'. She commented that the novel setting for using the target language made the pupils think in new ways about common topics such as the weather, shopping, travel, food and drink, and that using websites was particularly appealing for finding out new information. The theme was taught to three classes and, on the whole, boys performed better in French than they had previously, especially in terms of the presentation of their work, the accuracy and quality of their writing, and the care with and pride in what they were doing. There was also less of a difference in performance between the boys and the girls during all aspects of this work; the boys even wanted to carry on with the project when the time ran out.

Year 8 French

Theme: Les Caraïbes

Wize-up project which links several subjects:

Geography: Study of St Lucia.

History: Study of the slave trade.

French: Unit of work from *Camarades 2* based on personal details and centred on *La Martinique.*

Intro lesson on *La Martinique*: Background to the island, maps around the room, visual aids, etc, ideally at the same time as Geography starts its work.

2nd lesson in ICT room looking up info on *La Martinique*, finding five interesting facts about the island.

Some boys discovered nudist beaches and marked them on the maps, others found a bar run by Charlie, others discovered a cycle race and a motor bike convention, others were interested in zouk music and listened to it. More adventurous than the girls!

3rd lesson back in classroom compiling a phrase list based on *A la carte* sheet.

Both sheets to be stuck in exercise books and used as reference.

4th lesson view *Quinze minutes* video on Guadeloupe to get idea of the Frenchness. Listen for key phrases and note these – feedback to class.

5th lesson to go through writing frame discussing meaning. Begin to write own and include the facts they found – do in draft, go through with teacher to correct. Write up for Wize-up file.

Simple maps of *La Martinique* to be annotated, plotting main towns, sites of volcanoes, forests, etc.

In future have felt maps and key features like old *En Avant* maps and exploit.

Caribbean afternoon with a French presentation on *La Martinique.*

All pupils very interested, boys enjoyed the internet work and the video work.

Source: Margaret Turner, Hexham Middle School, Hexham

Pupil choice

A third subset of the first recommendation was to:

Create opportunities for an element of pupil choice in what is done in class and at home. This may help give pupils a greater sense of responsibility for what they do. **1a 3 8**

This recommendation resulted in a wide range of responses among teachers:

Strategies adopted to enable pupils to have some choice in lessons and at home included:

1 Giving Year 10 choice regarding what they did in a lesson. The teacher planned compulsory activities, which she presented as the *Menu du jour*, and others from which choices could be made, which were *A la carte*. The result, as reported by teachers and pupils, was that work was, on the whole, more willingly undertaken and more was done than was the case when all the work was decided in advance by the teacher. The terminology nicely linked initially with her topic of cafés and restaurants but was extended to other themes later.

2 Encouraging Year 10/11 choice within a coursework topic. As an example boys in one school preferred to produce a leaflet giving factual details about a town whereas the girls wanted to write a text explaining the pros and cons of living there. Both of course were acceptable; it was the production of a tangible, factual outcome which appealed to the boys in particular, whereas the girls appeared to enjoy deciding together what was good and what was not so good about where they lived.

3 For Friday afternoon lessons allowing pupils to choose how they wanted to spend the last fifteen minutes.

4 Allowing Years 10/11 choice of which aspects of a topic they would revise, followed up with an appropriately focused test. In this example the teacher kept a tally of which choices were made by the boys and which were made by the girls. In nearly all cases all were appropriate and were indications that both boys and girls were perceptively aware of what they needed to do in order to improve their performance. Encouraging individual learners to make decisions about what they needed to do seemed, on the whole, to lead to improved performance. This was particularly the case when, in one school, two after-school coursework clubs were started. The Year 11 were told they had to attend but that they could choose which one they went to. While this seemed to succeed a voluntary lunchtime club in another school was unsuccessful with decreasing numbers attending.

5 Having what different year groups talked about determined by chance. In one school the teacher prepared details of famous families from TV programmes and put these in a paper bag. During the lesson pupils picked a card from the bag, walked around the class asking carefully rehearsed questions to find the rest of their famous family, then, once together, introduced one member of the family from the details shown. The fact that chance had determined who got what was more engaging than having the teacher decide for them.

6 Developing greater learner autonomy by allowing pupils to choose the order, within a structured Scheme of Work, in which tasks were to be completed. Those which included an ICT element were more readily tackled by boys than others, and, interestingly, when boys were given the opportunity to write on the whiteboard they were more accurate than when they wrote on paper.

7 Devising a flexible homework policy/homework booklets with extension tasks. Many MFL staff in several schools adopted variations of this strategy.

    a Some experimented with lists of homework tasks to be completed by a set date within half a term but done when learners chose.

Source: Francis Dent, Ripley St Thomas High School, Ashton Road, Lancaster

Homework January–February 2003

There are six pieces of homework which must be completed by Friday February 14. You can do them at any point before this date. Hand the booklet in when it is complete

	Title	Description of task	Level you can achieve	Tick when complete
1.	*Mots coupés*	Match up the beginnings and endings of these French words – they are all school subjects.	1	
2.	*Au collège*	Read the six sentences describing people's likes and dislikes at school. Look at the grid below and in each column write the name of the person whose opinions are described there. **There are six names and seven columns – there will be a blank column when you have finished.**	3	
3.	*Comment trouves-tu ...?*	Write seven sentences describing how you feel about school subjects and how good you are at them.	3	
4.	*Qu'est-ce que tu penses de ...?*	Using the vocabulary on page 6, match up the English and French sentences. Write your answers in the box at the bottom of the page.	2	
5.	*Mon collège*	Read Pierre's letter about school and fill in the grid below in English.	4	
6.	*Mes matières*	Choose three school subjects and write three sentences on each one, in French, giving your opinion of them.	4	

Vocabulaire

Le français	French	Je suis fort(e) en	I am good at
L'allemand	German	Je ne suis pas fort(e) en	I am not very good at
L'espagnol	Spanish		
L'anglais	English	Je suis nul(le)	I am useless at
Les sciences	science	Je suis faible en	I am weak in
La physique	physics	Le prof	the teacher
La biologie	biology	Facile	easy
La chimie	chemistry	Important	important
Les maths	maths	Difficile	difficult
La religion	RE	Utile	useful
La technologie	technology	Intéressant	interesting
Le sport	PE	Nul	rubbish
L'éducation physique	PE	Ennuyeux	boring
L'informatique	IT	Sévère	strict
La géographie	geography	Sympa	nice
L'histoire	history	Ma matière préférée	my favourite subject
Le dessin	art		
La musique	music	Par contre	on the other hand
J'adore	I love/adore		
J'aime	I like	Bien sûr	of course
Je déteste	I hate		

MOTS COUPÉS

These words have been cut in half. Draw a line between beginnings and endings to get the complete words again. You can also colour them in, using a different colour for each word. (They are all school subjects.)

Au collège

Write each person's name in the column which best describes what they think of their subjects.

1. Béatrice aime l'allemand; elle n'aime pas le français.
2. Bernard aime les maths; il déteste l'éducation physique.
3. Thérèse adore les sciences; elle n'aime pas l'anglais
4. Thierry n'aime pas l'anglais; il déteste les sciences.
5. Sylvie déteste l'informatique; elle aime le français.
6. Sylvestre adore l'allemand; il adore l'informatique aussi.

✔	=	elle/il aime
✔✔	=	elle/il adore
✘	=	elle/il n'aime pas
✘✘	=	elle/il déteste

Opinion / Matière							
Allemand			✔	✔ ✔			
Anglais	✘	✔					✘✘
Éducation physique					✘✘		
Français			✘			✔	
Informatique		✔		✔✔		✘✘	
Maths					✘		
Sciences	✔✔						✘✘

Comment trouves-tu ...?

Give your opinion on seven subjects from the list below. For each sentence say what you think of the subject and then say how good you are at that subject.

For example:

J'adore l'histoire. Je ne suis pas fort en histoire.
(I love history. I am not very good at history.)

J'adore		le dessin le français le sport
J'aime		la biologie la géograhie la musique
Je n'aime pas		la physique la technologie l'anglais
Je déteste		l'espagnol l'histoire les maths

Je suis fort(e)		dessin français sport
Je ne suis pas fort(e)		biologie géographie musique
Je suis nul(le)	en	physique technologie anglais
Je suis faible		espagnol histoire maths

1. _____

2. _____

3. _____

4. _____

5. _____

6. _____

Qu'est-ce que tu penses de ...?

Match up the French and the English. Put the number of the matching English sentence in the box below. The first one is done for you.

	Français		Anglais
A	Je suis fort en anglais	1	*The teacher is strict*
B	C'est facile	2	*It is interesting*
C	Le prof est sévère	3	*I am good at English*
D	C'est difficile	4	*I love music*
E	C'est utile	5	*I hate maths*
F	C'est nul	6	*It is important*
G	C'est intéressant	7	*It is easy*
H	J'adore l'anglais	8	*The teacher is nice*
I	Je n'aime pas le dessin	9	*It is difficult*
J	Je déteste les maths	10	*It is boring*
K	J'aime la musique	11	*It is useful*
L	Le prof est sympa	12	*I don't like art*
M	C'est ennuyeux	13	*It is rubbish*
N	C'est important	14	*I love English*

A	3	B		C		D	
F		G		H		I	
J		K		L		M	
N		M					

Mon collège

Nancy le 6 Janvier

Cher Paul,
Merci de ta lettre. Je vais te parler un peu de mon collège.

J'aime le collège. Je fais beaucoup de matières. J'aime la biologie. Je suis fort en biologie, mais c'est difficile.

Ma matière préférée c'est maths. C'est très utile et le prof est sympa. L'anglais par contre est nul. Je suis faible en anglais et le prof est sévère.

J'adore le français bien sûr. C'est très important. Je suis fort en français.

Au revoir,

Pierre

Pierre talks about his school subjects and mentions four of them. Write what these subjects are in English, and give as much detail as you can about his opinions on these subjects.

Subject 1	Subject 2	Subject 3	Subject 4

Mes matières

Choose three school subjects and write three or four sentences on each one in French.

Use the vocabulary from *'Qu'est-ce que tu penses de …'* to help you.

Example:

> *J'adore la biologie. Le prof est sympa et c'est intéressant. Je suis fort en biologie.*

I adore biology. The teacher is nice and it is interesting. I am good at biology.

1.

2.

3.

Concours sur les devoirs

Fais ta selection de la liste suivante et écris le numéro et les instructions dans ton cahier ou sur ta feuille:

1   Je vais dessiner une image de ma trousse et du contenu.

2   Je vais écrire une bande dessinée avec des paroles en français dans des bulles comme celle de la page 12 dans le cahier d'exercices.

3   Je vais dessiner une carte de Noël en français.

4   Je vais dessiner un calendrier de dates importantes et personnelles, par exemple les anniversaires de ma famille et de mes amis.

5   Je vais écrire une lettre à mon correspondant/ma correspondante comme celle de la page 111 en *Métro 1*.

6   Je vais trouver une photo de ma maison et en faire une description comme celle de la page 74 en *Métro 1*.

7   Je vais écrire une liste de pays francophones et produire une carte du monde avec les noms des pays soulignés.

8   Je vais préparer une cassette pour parler des sports que j'aime et de ceux que je n'aime pas.

9   Je vais écrire une liste d'adjectifs avec des illustrations pour décrire mes amis/amies.

10   Je vais écrire un livre d'enfants sur l'alphabet français où chaque page aura une grande lettre suivie d'un mot et d'une illustration.

11   Je vais dessiner une famille et écrire une description de chaque membre.

12   Je vais écrire une conversation au sujet de frères et de sœurs.

13   Je vais composer un 'mots mêlés' pour un autre élève et y mettre les noms de quelques jours de la semaine/des couleurs, accompagné de la solution sur une autre feuille comme celle de la page 52 en *Métro 1*.

14   Je vais trouver une photo de moi et en faire une description comme celles des pages 31–33 en *Métro 1*.

15   Je vais trouver une photo d'un personnage célèbre et je vais en faire une description comme celle de la page 33 en *Métro 1*.

16   Je vais composer un jeu de société sur des personnages célèbres et leurs détails personnels.

17   Je vais dessiner des images d'animaux différents et en faire une description de chacun.

18   Je vais écrire un dépliant destiné aux touristes français qui visitent ma ville.

19   Je vais préparer un sondage sur les animaux domestiques.

20   Je vais faire un sondage des dates des anniversaires de chaque personne dans ma classe, puis en mettre les résultats au mur.

21   Je vais composer une chanson sur mes sports préférés et je vais l'enrégistrer.

22   Je vais composer un fomulaire à remplir sur un personnage célèbre.

23   Je vais faire une description de ma petite amie idéale/mon petit ami idéal et de ce qu'elle/il porte le weekend.

24   Je vais faire un calendrier illustré pour l'utiliser en classe.

25   Je vais préparer un bulletin météorologique comme ceux à la télé et je vais l'enrégistrer.

26   Je vais préparer un bulletin météorologique illustré avec des images qu'on peut utiliser en classe.

27   Je vais dessiner un poster de quelqu'un recherché par la police.

28   Je vais composer un jeu de société, avec des cartes illustrées, sur les sports.

29   Je vais faire un grand emploi de temps de ma classe, avec des images des matières, et je vais indiquer par ☺ ou ☒ celles que j'aime et celles que je n'aime pas.

30   Je vais composer un aide-mémoire de mots clefs et des phrases importantes du chapitre que je viens d'étudier.

BON POINT!

Nom:
Prénom:
Classe:

Pour sa participation dans le CONCOURS SUR LES DEVOIRS et obtenu le nombre de points suivants

pour la période entre
le _____
et
le_____

Ce bon point récompense tout l'effort fourni durant le premier module de *Métro*

Signature du professeur_____
Date_____

Source: Stephan Morris, Maelor School, Penley, Wrexham

b   One teacher with his Year 7 class, set some of his homeworks, as a *Concours sur les devoirs*. From a list of 30 possible tasks, linked to the textbook used by the school, one task had to be completed each half-term. Six were completed in each year and each led to the award of a certificate.

c   One teacher gave out a list to her Mixed Ability Year 8 of six possible homework titles. Every month pupils were asked to choose and complete three. The following example shows the nature of the differentiated tasks which were on offer. Within a theme of House and Home weaker pupils could choose to label rooms and furniture whereas more able learners could describe their home in a letter.

The assessment criteria were:
1 ambition (pupil self-assessment)
2 presentation (teacher assessed, but could be by peers)
3 accuracy (teacher assessed, but could be by peers)
Verbal comments in the target language were used for all three categories.

d   A teacher had pupils complete poems for homework and then read them onto cassette with background music, or as a rap. It was up to them to choose the way this was presented.

e   A PGCE student teacher teaching German invented a 'Homework Challenge'. From a list of 40 possible pieces of homework two had to be completed each fortnight on 'Homework Challenge' days. Of the 40 possibilities some were monthly tasks and had to be completed regularly; others were more open to pupil choice and included simple and harder tasks. Included in the list were written and oral activities. Two copies of the homework were given to the pupils, one to be stuck into their exercise books and one to be given to an adult at home. This helped ensure that parents knew what had been set and that also, if a child was absent from school, some work could be done at home if this was appropriate.

Mr Allen's Homework Challenge! Stick one copy into the front of your exercise book – the other must be handed to your parents

There are forty exercises below. Two exercises must be completed each fortnight on the "Homework Challenge" days. All exercises must be completed in German unless otherwise specified and handed into Mr Allen on time. Non-completed work will be completed during the following lunch hour. If this is not attended an after school detention will be issued. If there is any confusion about the exercises don't hesitate to approach Mr Allen as he will be happy to explain any questions. Do approach Mr Allen. Don't use the excuse that you didn't understand as it won't be accepted.

Once a month

1.   Choose ten German words to learn. Use the attached test page – remember to get your parents to sign the form to prove that you've learnt the words.

Ongoing: Begin at the beginning of the year and keep up to date each month

2.   Choose a *Bundesliga* team and follow their results throughout the season. Mr Allen could ask you at any time if they won or lost (see vocabulary sheet).

3.   Find a German penfriend and correspond using the internet. Exchange music, jokes, stories etc … Log onto www…de

***Einfach!* Simple exercises to attempt, shouldn't take too long**

4.   Find out and list all the German *Länder* and their capitals

5.   Make a card (birthday, Valentine's, Easter, Xmas)

6.   Make up a crossword in German

7.   Make up a quiz about Germany

8.   Make up a wordsearch

9.   Make up your own version of Blockbusters

10.   Write a list of famous German people

11.   Write a poem in German

12.   Write down some important dates (family birthdays or holidays)

13.   Write out a list of adjectives, illustrate them

Schwer! **More difficult exercises which will take longer and will require more preparation time.**

14.   Conduct a survey within your family or friends about what they think of each other

15.   Cut out an article from an English magazine and do a summary of it in German

16.   Describe and draw six different types of transport

17.   Describe what you did last weekend

18.   Describe your dream City team

19.   Describe your plans for the holidays

20.   Design a dream mode of transport

21.   Design an advertisement in German – poster, radio, T.V.

22.   Design and label a new football stadium for Bristol

23.   Design and label City's new football strip

24.   Design and label your dream campsite

25.   Draw a monster using the vocabulary learnt from parts of the body

26.   Find a photo of yourself and describe it

27.   Find a picture of a celebrity and describe it

28.   Find out information about Bristol and make a brochure of it

29.   Make a map of you local area

30.   Make a police 'wanted' poster for someone you know or a celebrity

31.   Plan a shopping spree for when you're a millionaire

32.   Plan a trip around the world

33.   Write out a dialogue of a conversation using the vocabulary we've learnt in class

34.   Write out a shopping list for presents for your family. Who is it for, where can you buy it from?

Mündlich! **Oral activities. Remember to request your tape from Mr Allen when attempting one of these exercises. If you have no recording equipment at home ask Mr Allen and he will organise some for you.**

35. Find and record some German music off the radio or internet. Mr Allen will then play it during the lesson. The rest of the class will evaluate it and give it marks out of ten.

36. Make a rap similar to that on *Hallo aus Berlin* and record it

37. Record a list of food and drink you like and why. Also include food and drink you don't like

38. Record a tape of all numbers up to 100. Also record 200, 300 … up to 1,000

39. Record a tape of the alphabet

40. Using the *Wurzels* CD write some lyrics in German and record it

Source: Ben Allen, PGCE Student, University of Bristol 2002–2003

Since the topic of flexible homework timetables and pupil choice was such a successful element in improving pupil performance this topic and its inspirational source will be explored in detail as one of the two detailed case studies which end this book. It is to Moira Edmunds, Support Teacher: Modern Languages, Angus Council, Scotland, that all credit and thanks are due for this element in the project.

2 What learners can tell us

2 Talking to the learners

Talk more to boys and girls of all ages about what makes or could make learning an MFL a positive, worthwhile and enjoyable experience. This might offer insights into how pupils define activities which are 'engaging', 'purposeful' and 'fun'. **3 6**

Talking to pupils became a productive strategy explored by a number of schools. Insights gained from the pupils, both boys and girls, did help formulate policies and in many cases provided teachers with alternative ways of teaching mixed gender classes. Actions included the following:

1 Within one MFL department all the teachers agreed questions for interviews with pupils about what they would like to learn within the topics in the school's Scheme of Work.

2 Several schools had a policy to set clear targets and objectives for each lesson. However, if rigidly followed at the beginning of every lesson this could become relatively meaningless and not allow for surprises and something unexpected. Some departments therefore made it policy to specify what was to be learned and achieved, not necessarily at the beginning, but certainly at some time within each lesson. Teachers found that if objectives were specified in written form the pupils could tick them off as they were completed, an activity which appealed to all pupils, especially boys, and demonstrated real short-term progress. Teachers reported that it was important to keep practice consistent within the MFL department, so that all pupils knew what to expect.

3 Some schools had policies to provide practical, friendly help to show boys **how to be organised** (keeping files, setting out work ...). This helped to demonstrate and exemplify MFL departmental expectations. A particularly helpful strategy especially for boys and also for many girls was to provide writing frames when setting written work, and showing how to revise both for school and GCSE examinations. Rather than this being an individual task, collaborative effort with a friend was sometimes found to be more productive than solo endeavour. In one school, what each pupil decided to do each week to improve was made public to the whole class and one pupil in turn kept a record of whether it had been done, or how much had been done. This check took place in front of the teacher but the teacher did not write what had been decided. Record keeping was done by a pupil in charge of a log book, which was kept safe by the teacher.

4 Schools allocated time in a lesson to allow pupils to move about, engage in something physical, play a game using dice, cards, counters, find information, discuss a task. This was especially popular with boys and, provided it was an integral part of the lesson, was rarely abused. It allowed discussion, movement and comparison of work, an aspect which one boy explained as being an integral part of, for example, science lessons which made these lessons more active, more practical and thus more engaging.

5   Teachers provided competition but against 'personal bests', rather than against others. Examples included precisely timed competitive activities such as 'how many words on x can you recall in 60 seconds?' The emphasis on collaborative work rather than the idea of 'winners and losers' was particularly effective in motivating less able learners – both boys and girls – and did not reinforce the fact that they were 'losers' in comparison with more able peers.

6   Certification for short-term goals was seen by all teachers and schools who adopted the practice to be a strong motivator, helping all pupils see their progress and have it recognised officially. The certificate illustrated below shows what has been completed successfully on the aspects to be consolidated and improved on the back.

> has successfully
> completed
> Module 1
> of Oakfield School
> Year 7
> French Course.
>
> This covers the following:
> ★ Naming School subjects
> ★ Saying you like or dislike them
> ★ Giving a reason
> ★ Using some reflexive verbs
> ★ Describing a typical day

Source: Lesley Hooper, Oakfield school, Frome, Somerset

French review sheet   Name: Date:

Year 7 Module 1: Ma journée

Aims of the module:

- to be able to talk about your likes and dislikes at school;
- to give your opinions about subjects;
- to talk about your timetable;
- to be able to use some quantifiers;
- to describe a typical day;
- to be able to use some reflexive verbs;
- to be able to use some regular "er" verbs.

Target:

✔ Ask and answer questions about school subjects and your timetable
   3 questions and answers = S3
   4 questions and answers = S4

✔ Write down your opinions about subjects, giving reasons why you like or dislike them
   Write using a wordlist and your exercise book notes = W3
   Write from memory = W4

Pupil review:

☺

Teacher review:

☺

To improve further …

☞

Source: Lesley Hooper, Oakfield school, Frome, Somerset

7   The use of frequent, but focused praise, delivered discreetly and not in public, for a range of criteria (organisational skills, effort, willingness, participation, presentation, pronunciation, fluency, accuracy …); together with the award of badges and stickers effectively allowed recognition of achievement in many of its aspects. Examples in French might include *Bon effort! Belle présentation! Bonne prononciation! Bonne participation!*

8   And finally, taken from Ted Wragg, *Times Educational Supplement* (16 May 1997: 5) basing lessons on three elements 'humour, adventure, sport'.

Helping learners learn

> *Trial and evaluate ideas designed to involve pupils more actively in their learning not only in the choice of content but also how to go about their learning – classwork activities (successfully completing listening tasks, adopting appropriate reading strategies, improving the quality of their writing, speaking), homework, memorising, independent study etc.* **1a 1c 1e 1f 1g 1h 2 3 6 7**

Every learner is different and many approach what they have to do in a variety of ways, some of which are efficient and some less so. Boys in the research project often remarked that they were unsure how to go about some of the tasks which they were set, including how to learn language by heart, for tests, for revision, etc; or what to do when they were listening to a cassette. They were also unclear as to the purposes of some of the activities which teachers asked them to do in Modern Language lessons such as engage in choral repetition. Perhaps practising more discreetly with a partner would be less threatening for some. Why should they be encouraged to answer questions rapidly in front of the class? For some confident pupils this might be fine but for the more timid or hesitant could they not try out an answer with a partner first before being asked to perform in public? An awareness of some of these elements of lessons which were particular to modern language learning prompted some teachers to explore in more detail what pupils felt about what they were being asked to do, what the learning purposes were, how best to go about certain tasks, etc. They decided either as individuals but more often as a departmental initiative to:

1   Share good ideas from learners about:

- how they learn best;
- how they go about tasks;
- what for the pupils was successful practice; this was particularly revealing if expressed in their own words;
- how they went about and what they did when redrafting work (solo, in pairs, groups …);
- preferences about resources, using e-mail, using audio tapes, accessing sources of help;
- comparing and evaluating which form of presentation is most effective. Boys and girls in one school evaluated which of two PowerPoint presentations helped them to understand best how to tell the time in French.

Some teachers spoke regularly to pupils in or out of class time and then explored some of their practical suggestions with targeted classes in the school. Particularly successful projects involved looking at and evaluating ways pupils went about 'learning homeworks'; asking learners to invent their own ways of helping their learning such as playing music with a fast beat when tests were taking place and music with a slow beat accompanying committing words, phrases, sentences to memory; creating 'thinking time' before answering questions orally in class; how pupils approached checking work; what pupils found most helpful in helping them learn and what worked best for them; what strategies boys invented – and shared – for remembering words, phrases, e.g. based, in one instance, on a complex and often funny association with English words and rhyming slang.

In the longer term some teachers decided to set up a website WebBoard with a discussion forum, to exchange ideas, good practice and resources.

2   Other projects involved:

- discovering more about learners' preferred learning styles, with a focus on kinaesthetic learning, and producing resources for this such as letters on movable cards to show where to place plural markers and endings; word cards on a washing line to create new sentences or to add a new element of language (adjective, connective); parts of sentences on cards to show changes of word order.

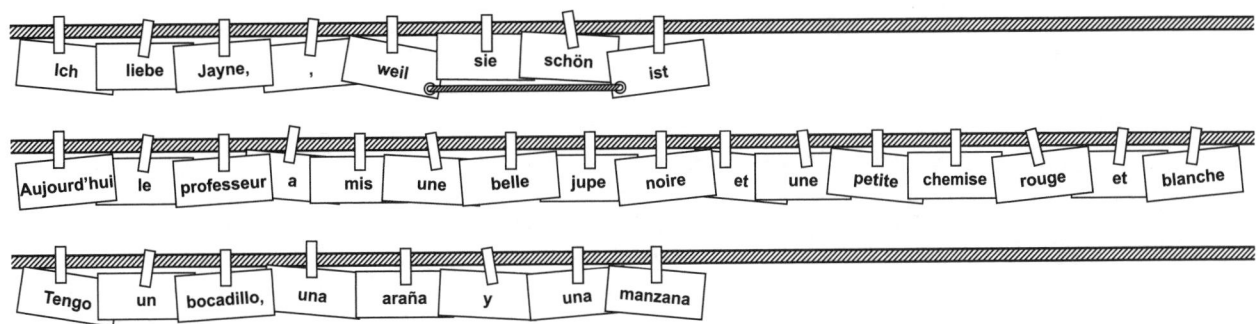

- encouraging active, physical ways to explore elements of grammar; example: the teacher calls out an infinitive and pupils jump on coloured mats in the gym according to how the perfect tense is formed – blue mats for verbs in French which make their perfect tense with *avoir* and red mats for verbs which take *être*; or for German nouns the teacher calls out the noun with no gender marker and pupils jump on blue mats for masculine words, red for feminine words and brown for neuter words …

3   In another experiment boys – and girls – decided on key words they needed to know for GCSE topics, and displayed these – word-processed and checked by teacher – on cards in the classroom as a reference source and on laminated 'placemats' for each table in the classroom at the beginning of and during the teaching of every topic.

4   Other projects had a clear focus on helping boys improve their handwriting, given a marked correlation between neat presentation and accuracy in the foreign language.

5   Some teachers decided to change the layout of the classroom (horseshoe, circle, semi-circle …), the location of a lesson (ICT room, hall, field, playground, wood …) as appropriate for different activities. This not only made the lessons more varied but was more appropriate for some activities.

3 Making the learning purposes clear

3 Explaining teacher intentions

Teachers can make more explicit from the first year of language study why they are asking learners to do what they include in lesson time and for homework – and what the teacher sees as the purpose of each activity (choral repetition, pairwork, writing tasks, listening to cassettes …) in terms of developing and improving language performance. This may help involve learners more in the teaching and learning process, demystify aspects of MFL lessons and explain the precise purpose of what pupils are asked to do.
3 6 7

This recommendation is clearly linked to much of what has just been discussed. There were clear points for action here, and teachers decided to:

1   Make explicit the reason for and justify each activity done in class in language learning terms.

2   Have their pupils explain in lessons, in English, exactly what they had to do and how it helped their learning.

3   Ask groups of boys and girls working in mixed gender groups to explain in their own words how the language they are learning 'fits together'. However, in one school, the girls reported that after a while girls resented the helper role. As a consequence the school decided on some occasions groups would work as single sex groups, on others in mixed groupings.

4 Language models and instructions

4 Repeating language models, explanations and instructions

If a teacher provides a language model for pupils to follow and use later, it is helpful if this is repeated to the whole class and to individuals at several different moments in a lesson. Giving instructions and explanations a number of times may help when a lack of concentration or bewilderment prevents these being understood when first presented. Boys also suggested that if instructions and explanations were made interactive they understood them better. **9 10**

This was seen by many teachers as a key element in establishing the successfulness of a Modern Language lesson and one which was particular to modern languages, given that the language to be practised and used by the pupils comes mainly from the teacher and that instructions and often explanations are, in most classrooms, delivered through the target language. Decisions were made as follows:

1 To start the lesson with a pupil-focused activity, or include a pupil-focused activity within the first five minutes of a lesson; asking how they are, what they did yesterday, what they like, what they had for breakfast, how they came to school, what they will do in the evening, etc.

2 To plan activities to last for approximately five minutes to minimise the short attention span of some pupils and have each build on and repeat parts of what had gone before.

3 When writing on the board stop in the middle of a word/sentence, turn to the class and ask what letter/word comes next, to predict content, ensure attention, engage the group.

4 When starting on a new topic, display key words, or phrases, clearly on cards. These can be used as a reference source, an aid to recall, a framework for telling a story or for recreating the language being taught. Not only does the display become interactive but boys in particular have said how much this kind of framework or structure helps them remember what they have to learn. If the display remains on the wall it also helps those who forget easily.

5 When setting objectives display these on slips of paper so that pupils, by agreement with others in the class, can tick them off as they are completed. This ensures not only that they have been understood by individuals but that the rest of the class is involved in the decision.

6 When giving instructions and setting up tasks make clear what is expected and what is needed to complete the activity.

M	Materials – what is needed
I	In or out of seats
N	Noise level – whether the activity is in silence or whether talking is allowed
T	Time – how long the activity should take
O	Objectives – why/how what is being taught will enable the task to be completed

Source: Marie Mills, Durham Johnston Comprehensive School, Durham

5 Keeping up, catching up

5 Preventing a downward spiral

Provide strategies for pupils to catch up or keep up by trialling directed or independent study in school, precise and limited targets, self-help using supplementary material, work with a Foreign Language Assistant, extra individual guidance from a MFL teacher, departmental MFL 'surgery' times. Some of these strategies may not only prevent a downward spiral but help make learners more responsible for their improvement.
1e 7 9 10

In MFL lessons keeping the attention of learners is critical especially at the beginning when the language needed for subsequent activities is presented and modelled. If learners miss the initial stage they are at a loss; they may neither know what to do nor what language to use. Over time the situation can develop where learners feel that to catch up is impossible. To help put this right there are two possible strategies. The first is for teachers and other learners to repeat both the instruction and the language needed to carry it out at different times and in different forms during the lesson. The second is for the MFL department to organise surgeries where extra and focused help can be provided. Most of the teachers who organised surgeries started them for Year 10, where students came for guidance on a weekly basis. Others decided that an earlier start was necessary and organised them for Years 7 and 8. For learners doing their GCSE, surgeries were designed to offer weekly help with GCSE coursework and to set and agree weekly targets. In one school this improved boys' grades so that all boys scored C grades and above. Most were run by members of the MFL department, Sixth form students (on a voluntary basis) and/or the Foreign Language Assistant. Perhaps not unexpectedly some pupils preferred to go to their own teacher and some to someone different.

1   In one school surgeries were replaced by 'Pop in', 'Chat' slots because when the teacher set up surgeries for Year 11 the boys said they wanted a less formal meeting, more of a chat. As a result the teacher said that they could meet 'when she was around' – which she engineered – and boys came more regularly. Teachers also asked girls to help the boys during pop in times, although this had to be done very casually with suggestions like 'Girls, I don't suppose you could give these lads a hand …' Normally the strategy worked quite well. However, as another school reported – and we showed earlier – involving girls was not always productive since some became tired of their helper role. One teacher summed up the advantages and disadvantages succinctly as:

Language Surgery

Advantages

- Get to see who is struggling and who feels that they are struggling.

- Helps students to keep up with the work.

Disadvantages

- Some simply pop in for a chat and to keep out of the cold.

- Some weeks no one comes along – dead time.

Source: Chris Williams, St Thomas More RC School, North Shields

---

2 Other catching up opportunities included:

a For every topic at GCSE a set of vocabulary/expression cards, the target language on one side and English on the other. Prior to a topic being introduced these were passed around the class, each pupil reading the card, passing it on, then trying a timed spelling game; a correct spelling scores +1, an incorrect scores –1. As the topic progressed these cards were available in the classroom at any time for revision, checking, etc. Resources such as these were often produced collaboratively by a TA (teaching assistant), a Foreign Language Assistant, or by other students.

b A display of topic-based reading (charts, posters, cards) in the classroom. To assess how often these were used pupils were asked to log what they had consulted.

6 First foreign language and second foreign language learning

> **6 The relationship between learning a first and a second foreign language**
>
> *Since boys see learning a second foreign language is not necessarily made easier by their experience of learning a first foreign language teachers could make more explicit links between the two. This may help explore and recognise similarities, where they exist, as well as illustrate significant differences. It was useful at times to compare mother tongue and the target languages.* **13**

There were no projects which explored this recommendation.

7 Working together: Modern Foreign Language departmental strategies

Acknowledging achievement

1   In many schools there are non-subject specific schemes in place to reward achievement. Some MFL teachers decided that these could be used without any amendment to help motivation in MFL. Other teachers, however, decided that Modern Language specific rewards were needed because by the nature of the subject short-term as well as long-term achievement required systematic recognition. All agreed that although boys liked receiving praise and rewards, teachers should avoid making a public display of recognising success and always try to interact with individuals on a one-to-one basis. Strategies for rewarding achievement included:

   a   Giving two cinema tickets for the highest number of Merit Marks gained by pupils. In one town, when approached by the MFL teacher, the manager of a local cinema complex donated two free tickets because of his wish to promote foreign language learning. He also believed that the two recipients would spend enough on snacks to compensate for his loss of income!

   b   Acknowledging success with Reward Stickers. Even older pupils, especially boys, were keen on collecting these.

   c   Acknowledging good work/effort. A slip of paper with child's name on it went into a raffle bin. A draw took place at the end of the lesson to select the daily champion and these names then went forward for a half-termly prize draw

   d   Rewarding good work with a 'praise card' which was the system in place throughout the school; ten 'praise cards' resulted in a postcard being sent home.

   e   Acknowledging good work/effort by *bons points*, which in turn led to the award of raffle tickets. This system operated with different coloured raffle tickets for each year and all departmental staff were involved in the draw.

   NB It is important that all learners gain *bons points* for some aspect of their work; otherwise, if there are winners there will be losers – often boys – who will lose further confidence and self-esteem.

2   Another strategy found to be motivating was for a department (and the school) to set up a system of end-of-Module certificates, awarded termly, which recorded an individual

learner meeting a number of specified targets. In one instance pupils assessed themselves against clearly specified learning objectives in the form of 'I can ...' statements in the target language. The teacher then added a comment. Boys, particularly, focused on the competitive nature of the project and were proud of their demonstrable progress, especially if achievement cards were used, on which short-term achievement statements could be ticked off – or marked with coloured stickers or dots. They needed some graphic representation – such as graphs showing results (hopefully improving) in writing – to show them how well they were doing. Teachers who explored this idea found it worked best if they started with pupils in their first year of foreign language learning.

3   Modern language learning is perceived by many learners as being more demanding than other subjects. In addition, if the course is seen by pupils as only compulsory in Key Stage 3, therefore lasting only three years, many, even good linguists, when given the option, may choose to drop the subject. With this once prohibited possibility now becoming a reality there is a fall in numbers of post-14 pupils – especially boys – in some secondary schools who continue with their study of a foreign language. Recognising this as a potential threat to first – and second – foreign language provision some teachers decided to provide intensive language learning (e.g., a 30 hour intensive Spanish course) for those willing to learn. Volunteers were, in one case, in Year 6, aged ten, and in another school post-16 students. In this way teaching expertise was not lost with decreasing numbers in Key Stage 4 but was used elsewhere in the same or other local schools. Perhaps significantly boys in these classes appeared more willing to opt for shorter, limited time courses, especially when the language being learnt was not French or German. Although further research and experimentation are needed before findings of this sort are used as the basis for policy decisions it is perhaps significant that short-term, focused foreign language learning attracts boys, as well as girls. With the publication of the *Languages Ladder* (2005) assessment in 23 different languages will be available by 2006/07. This should help make all learners aware – and proud – that they can achieve success. It should also demonstrate that what they achieve has status outside the classroom.

Linked to this is the last recommendation in *Boys' performance in MFL*, namely that the motivation of boys and of girls to learn a foreign language can be enhanced:

Focusing on the benefits of learning a foreign language

> *By achieving a high status and visible profile for languages within the school and by establishing live links with the local community and with foreign speakers.* **T**

Many schools, long before the appearance of this publication, already had a high profile for MFL and links of this sort firmly in place. The list which follows may, however, serve as a prompt for discussion. Within the projects reported on here some schools made the decision to do the following as school policy.

1   Display MFL signs throughout the school to include:

- signs on classrooms;
- signs in corridors (colour-coded for language);
- signs for Subject Areas.

In one instance it was Year 10 boys who made the signs in Design and Technology. The appropriate language was provided by parents, teachers and a Modern Languages' adviser who sent templates to schools in her area.

2   Set up in-school bulletin/notice boards for pupil-to-pupil communication and reader responses. Some featured work of the month, others advertisements and 'for sale' items. There were also descriptions of exchange visits used as publicity and accompanying question sheets. These sheets were an important element of the display. They encouraged other pupils to see what was there; if they wanted more information they could send a message to the named individual contributors, ask questions, respond to 'for sale' notices or answer quiz questions.

3   To make pupils aware of the usefulness of learning a foreign language. This was – and still is – a feature of the school's career guidance. The Head of Department invites students who have recently left school as well as adults who use a MFL in their job to talk to whole year groups in school. Each speaker describes how he or she uses a foreign language in work. The most persuasive event was when he invited a past, 'not very good' student to say why he wished he had done better and worked harder in his French lessons at school. This talk was particularly successful because the use of the foreign language was modest and therefore seen to be achievable; the past student was by then a lorry driver making frequent trips to Belgium, France and beyond.

4   To agree within a MFL department five questions which any class can ask any visitor who comes into a MFL teaching room. These are displayed as flashcards on the wall in the appropriate foreign language. As a visitor to this classroom I can bear witness to the power a class feels when they discover they can ask a total stranger questions in French and – hopefully – understand the responses. This project was developed in a Middle School and has now been replicated several times.

5   To mount MFL displays around the school. This is certainly not a new idea but making the wall displays in classrooms interactive certainly created interest. A feature of the descriptions of trips abroad already mentioned was to make it policy to:

a   encourage reader responses and questions, etc, to the writers and originators of the display;

b   have twenty words/expressions within any display on a range of topics which can be learned by groups of children. Each pupil learns five words and at the end of, say, five minutes (timed with a stop watch) the group has to produce all twenty. This can be used by any small group of children within any class. It seems to work best with groups of four.

As an activity for pupils who finish an activity early – from any class – it is always useful to have language on display for these quick workers to learn.

6   To organise a Modern Languages/European evening to raise the profile of MFL within the community. One school made it their policy to involve different groups in staging a performance, serving food and drink, and conducting role plays at parents' evenings. Visitors were often very impressed by their children's enthusiasm, good pronunciation, fluency, etc, which they had seldom seen before!

7   To create the possibility in a school for pupils to 'Teach a Friend a Language' (TAFAL). This was a scheme in which a pupil with one home language taught a volunteer friend that language, regularly once a week in lunchtime, for a term. Results were impressive; in 2005, 41 pairs of pupils learnt a new language, with 21 languages being taught and learnt in this way. At the end of the term each couple was judged and their achievement rewarded. This project won a European Award for Languages, a major achievement worth celebrating, and one which involved fifteen pairs of boys! (See **www.cilt.org.uk/promoting/resources/index.htm#tafal** for further details.)

Part 2

Participating schools:
Particular practices

8

How the projects came about and developed

Notes on the participating schools and how teachers became involved

The eight groups have different histories. In Somerset twelve teachers attended a meeting arranged by the county School Development Adviser on 30 November 2001, and expressed an interest in putting into practice projects either as a personal initiative or as the result of a departmental decision. In October 2002, ten of the Somerset teachers had projects underway, seven of which were described and illustrated at the first of two follow-up meetings held on 17 October 2002 and during a second meeting on18 June 2003.

In Leicestershire six teachers attended an initial presentation in December 2001 in a county residential centre, and in February 2002, four reported active involvement in projects in their schools. These teachers reported on progress on 13 March 2003, at a meeting organised by the co-ordinator of the Leicestershire Comenius Centre.

In Essex a presentation was made on 5 March 2002, at the invitation of a Head of Department in an Essex Secondary school; four members of its MFL department, and a student teacher on school placement were present as were eight teachers and one student teacher from eight local schools. As far as can be discovered a total of six teachers were engaged in projects.

On 15 March 2002, the Head of the MFL Department in a Language College in Carlisle organised a presentation held on the Carlisle Campus of St Martin's College. The twenty four teachers present proposed twelve separate but collaborative initiatives. In February 2003, eight teachers had eleven projects in progress, most of whom reported at a meeting organised by the co-ordinator of the North West Comenius Centre in Lancaster on 12 March 2003.

A fifth regional group attended an introductory meeting held in November 2002, at the North East Comenius Centre in Sunderland, organised by the then centre co-ordinator. Eighteen schools were represented and nineteen teachers present. Participants formulated action plans and reported at a follow-up session on 21 March 2003.

The sixth group of thirty five PGCE student teachers and thirty teachers, many of whom were mentors (Associate Tutors) to the PGCE students present, and four university MFL teacher-trainer tutors met in Bristol University on 16 January 2003. A follow-up reporting session took place on18 June 2003.

The seventh and eight groups were based in South and North Wales. Introductory meetings took place in Cardiff and Bangor on 3 July 2003 and 2 July 2004, respectively, with follow-up meetings on 5 December 2003 and 3 December 2004. Twelve and four teachers attended the two first sessions and thirteen and two the follow-up, others having launched projects but not always able to attend the second meeting.

Individual teachers who contributed to sessions on 'improving boys' performance in MFL', or who worked with the author in other contexts were also extremely influential in writing this book. It is to all these professionals that I owe a huge debt of gratitude.

An extended project

9

A case study of work carried out by Dirk Pereira, St Neots Community School, St Neots, Cambridgeshire

Introduction

This case study offers insights into the way a Head of Modern Languages in a 1,000+ secondary school broadened the debate about teaching Modern Languages into strategies designed to create a positive ethos in school towards learning and schooling in general. Much of what follows applies to MFL teaching and learning. It has particular relevance to teaching less willing boys and girls and is included here for discussion. The study is based on an extended interview in school where the teacher describes and illustrates his practice. Many aspects of his practice were also observed working. Present at the interview (which was audio-recorded and from which quotation is taken) were two newly qualified teachers and one trainee teacher who all, in varying degrees, had been able to implement much of the policy and practice explored here. Key questions and key aspects of the discussion are shown by headings in bold. Where actual words in the quotations have been altered or are summarised these are shown in square brackets to help readers follow the sense of what was said.

How do we transform learning? How to create a climate for creative learning?

At the beginning of the school year, and at times during the year, a whole year group is brought together in a open-plan teaching area. This is a deliberate policy designed to encourage a climate for learning with pupils assuming personal responsibility for what they do in school and at home. The teacher explained:

*We asked the students, and a hundred of them would be out in the area – four groups doing French, four groups doing German in each year group – we asked them 'Why are **you** here?', Why are **we** here?' – a bit of a religious question, metaphysical in a sense.*

From this discussion and from students' written contributions (some quotations from the students are used in group or individual discussions later on) ideas from the students about learning, working, getting on with people, etc, were noted. The first time the teacher explored the potential of this approach was in his previous school. At the time the teacher grouped the students' ideas under three key words, **care, dignity and respect**. He had then encouraged a boy, a Year 10 student who was a good artist, to produce a poster which showed in cartoon form examples from the whole year discussion. The poster illustrated what each of these three words meant in terms of day-to-day being and working together. This was known as The Learning Poster. It showed eight cartoons with captions such as 'No bullying', 'No put-downs', 'Please use positive language', 'No litter', etc. The practice, as he explained, was now being used in his present school, where he is Head of Department.

We ask the students which one of those things is the most important for us. We use this poster quite a lot. We're trying to get students to turn it round and for them to be teachers and us to be learners.

The teacher and the year group created this climate for learning by exploring the two elements of **care** and **respect** in detail with reference to the cartoons on the Learning Poster. The word 'dignity' had been taken away because, as the teacher admitted:

… it's a very hard one even for adults to understand.

This discussion takes time because pupils want to offer different interpretations. However, if a pupil says, as indeed one did

Oh, that's the most important, Sir – 'no litter' – …

the teacher would relate the comment, where appropriate, to the two key words. In this instance the teacher said:

*No litter, but that's to do with **care** and **respect**, isn't it?*

Since all the pupils suggestions were, and were shown to be related to care and respect the teacher came to an agreement with the year group that these were key. As he said to the pupils:

Everyone should be treated with care and respect, including all the staff, cleaners, visitors, office staff, support staff. That's what we mean by 'everyone'. And we have the right to feel safe and comfortable in our environment, i.e. no bullying or put-downs.

In the discussion with the year group the teacher also made reference to the pupils' emotional intelligence, an area which he explores in detail later. This, he feels, is a basic element in motivation and willingness to learn, acknowledging to the interviewer that his thinking has been influenced in particular by the work of Goleman (see inter alia Goleman 1996). As he explained to the pupils:

*We can't work, can we, if we're angry; [if we are angry] we can't do maths. So, care and respect, the right to be safe and comfortable [are key] – everyone has a right to learn. We agreed those principles and premises. And then, should a child be recalcitrant, throw something at someone, call someone a name […] the teacher doesn't have to get angry. He might say to Johnny, who has got angry 'Hang on, I thought, Johnny, we'd agreed something fairly early on in front of the whole year group, didn't we? Throwing something doesn't make people feel safe or give everyone the right to learn'. Or "You're not really showing care and respect are you?' Or 'Am I wrong, Johnny? Sorry. I mean I shouldn't be saying this. **You** tell me what **you** are feeling?' Turning it round. Johnny will then have to remember what we've all agreed and, in fact, it's not a telling-off process, it's Johnny reassessing his behaviour and having a chance to put his own thoughts into place to give himself the new chance, the blank slate, to start afresh, but with no one putting him down. If we're asking children not to put people down, why an earth are we still shouting and screaming at children in our classrooms every day. I would advocate that (as) the cane was banned, we should ban aggressive shouting in classrooms.*

His approach with the pupils is to reverse roles. He is explicit about this and tells them that although his job is that of a teacher his role is that of a learner.

He has firmly held beliefs about classrooms and the use of desks; committing people to sit behind desks he believes creates physical and psychological barriers. He links this to how we learn: *75% of our time is not with pens and paper. So why do we have desks? Why do we have tables?*

When he talks the pupils through questions such as these, as well as broad issues mentioned before – **why are we here? what do we want out of this (experience)?** – he builds on the pupils' responses and asks them to explore the practical implications of their suggestions.

Right. OK. That's a nice idea. How can we bring that idea to fruition.

He reinforces the statement that the pupils are the teachers and the teachers are the learners.

He also takes care to accommodate a variety of learning styles when deciding with the group what is appropriate action.

We have to learn about Jenny's kinaesthetic style, Jamie's auditory style, Sarah's mixture of all three styles, what is behind this learning and thinking process, the cognitive skills.

Having ensured consensus he concluded:

Right. That's an agreed set of premises and we all agree.

The demands of learning

He is careful to explain to the year group that learning is not always easy:

We say that every invitation to learn is an invitation to take risks, to be uncomfortable for a while, to be voluntarily incompetent.

His thinking here is based on the work of John McGuiness (see inter alia Robson and McGuiness 1999). As he says:

I use this [statement] a lot with trainee teachers in particular and in work with the NQTs […] I think that it's an encapsulation of a huge amount of things, that phrase. You can really take [it] apart. It's quite powerful in French and German as well.

The teacher then explores what risk-taking means in the context of learning a Modern Foreign Language. For him this is the willingness to make mistakes.

Because when we jump over this line, we are uncomfortable … whenever we do something for the first time … I've just come back from skiing, as you can see. But three years ago I wasn't a skier and now I'm much more comfortable. I was scared stiff the first time up the mountain. I was learning. But we have to put ourselves into this incompetence voluntarily, don't we? So how do we bring this climate about? How do we get our children to jump off that cliff? We say:

- *Well, do you remember two weeks ago I gave you a parachute?*

- *[A boy's words] Oh yes, Sir, right. Well, what if the parachute don't open, Sir?*

- *Oh, there's another one inside your pack. That was the four-weeks-ago-set-of-words.*

- *Yeah, but what if that don't open, both of them?*

- *We'll look underneath. Look over the cliff. You've got a safety net. That was the six-weeks-ago work.*

- *Yeah, I might fall through it, Sir.*

- *Yeah, but look underneath, there's a mattress. That was the two-months-ago work.*

- *Oh right, yeah.*

And suddenly we are creating these feelings of 'Yeah, I might want to jump. Show me the next line. I want to jump. Show me the next line'. And where do we go with those sorts of ideas? We say to the students […] if they wish to accept the invitation. Great. We'll really help you, if you want. We can't teach you anything but we can help you learn, if you want to. If you wish to accept that, great. If you don't, your choice, stay outside and we'll come and give you some work, obviously because we have to, but you'll probably be by yourself in a room without your mates. Why am I here?' Turn it round. 'Why are you here?' and we'll see some of the answers that the students have given as to why they're here later.

Emotional intelligence: An alternative criterion for success

I've been working in emotional intelligence for some time now. These wonderful phrases 'Conscientiousness and integrity', 'Decisiveness', etc. Why don't we start rewarding our students for [actually] coming into school when their mum and dad have split up the night before, when their uncle has died of cancer. Instead, we give them a test, don't we? We say, 'Do these CATS test'. Then we identify those students through [the] CATS test [score] and SATS for the rest of their schooling. Instead of saying, 'Well done for motivating yourself, for having this self-awareness, for being emotional(ly) resilient enough to come into school', we mark them out of ten.'

I'm [also] working with an Occupational Psychologist from the Papworth Trust who's written lots of papers. He's wanting to come in and do some work with the students because no one's actually done any work with students before. They've done it with bankers, pilots, adults in work. [They've looked at] appraisal, how we appraise each other [using] emotional intelligence instead of normal appraisal situations. Knowing that 40% of us who go through an appraisal will hate it, knowing that when we come out of an appraisal, we normally want to hit someone, so, knowing this as adults, why are we doing this with our children still?

How are they appraising themselves? Are they appraising themselves? When do they appraise themselves? Shouldn't we be turning it around and making people comfortable – that word again – with their own appraisals, [with] them knowing how you move the next step up, knowing where you are now, where we are, why we are here [...] again a bit of a religious context.

Peer and self-assessment

The MFL department has a common policy on self and peer assessment which is used at the end of every lesson. Each pupil awards him or herself a number, 1, 2, 3 or 4, in the target language for their performance during the lesson:

Ein, zwei, drei oder vier at the end of each lesson – students' self-assessment.

The marks are quickly noted in a markbook by the teacher and enable progress to be charted by pupil and teacher alike. This is done in public. The teacher explains:

'One' means 'I have performed excellently, fantastisch at the end of the lesson and I will give myself this mark'. 'Two' means 'I've done a good performance' – whatever that might mean per student because we're all different with our own criteria, emotionally. It doesn't mean that I've put my hand up three times because that might be good for Johnny but it might be awful for Sara who normally does it twenty times in the lesson. Johnny might never have put his hand up. The first time in the term he does – wonderful – let's celebrate that. So 'three' would be 'I can improve a little bit for next lesson' and 'four' would be 'I must improve an awful lot for next lesson.' So, in German these are:

1 *fantastisch*
2 *gut*
3 *ich kann ein bisschen besser machen*
4 *ich muss viel, viel besser machen*

As the teacher pointed out, for an eleven year-old, a twelve year-old, or a sixteen year-old pupil to analyse their own performance in public and to give themselves a mark at the end of a lesson demands an honest self appraisal. It also makes them consider the criteria they are using, especially since they may be asked, by either the teacher or someone else in the group, to justify the mark and to say why it is a true reflection of their performance. The teacher cites an example of a discussion where the teacher and a pupil differ in their assessment. The class is a difficult Year 8 class and the pupil is Chesney.

[Chesney thinks] she is fantastisch *[…] If I disagree, I just raise my eyebrow and she will have to reassess. If we're still in disagreement I say to the LSA (Learning Support Assistant) 'Frau Brown, ein, zwei, drei oder vier für Chesney?' 'Oh zwei' So the LSA's brought in. If we're still in disagreement and Chesney still doesn't agree, I say, 'What about the rest of the class' 'Die Klasse, ein, zwei, drei oder vier?' and the class chimes in.*

The teacher is careful to point out that the system has limitations:

Normally we find the students actually put themselves down of course. They do not want to say they are excellent. The silent majority never says 'I am excellent'. How do we get the silent majority to own up to their excellence? [We have to] turn it round, this anti-culture. Turning it round […] Promote the idea that the silent majority is excellent and it's only the one or two who stop the lesson.

In order to reinforce success parents are shown this pupil profile, normally at a Parents' Evening; they are frequently surprised.

When you show parents this, at a parents' evening – the profile of their student's success – they think, 'Crikey, I can't do that on my days' work. I'd lie'. This is what we're all about […] honesty, and self-awareness, where we are in the class at this time …

With one exception all members of the MFL department, including two newly qualified Teachers in their first year of teaching, and a trainee teacher from Cambridge University's Faculty of Education have operated the self-assessment system which was started in Year 7. There is the expectation in the department that it will continue throughout a pupil's schooling, as it did in the head of department's previous school.

The performance of each individual in each class is also regularly recorded on video and is used to show improvement, or otherwise, by the teacher. The whole-class video is also the evidence on which a whole-class mark is awarded. This mark is normally given by another class who look at the video and make an assessment of the group performance. In this way the dynamic changes from a focus on the individual to a focus on the class and is done explicitly to reinforce the idea that an individual's actions, behaviour, and performance, impinge on and influence others in the group.

Success and motivation

The teacher describes how the system of self-assessment marks helps motivation. He describes a very difficult Year 9 class.

There's honesty there. It's not saying 'I'm excellent' all the time. But [I will say] if you are wanting to improve and your next lesson is a 'one', then you will have improved. What more can you ask a student to do? And when you show this to parents they are so gob smacked that Damien improved in the next lesson when he said he wanted to. 'My son did that?'

Self-assessment leads on to wider issues, gradually introduced as and when the class and group discussion make them relevant and appropriate. Underpinning all is the teacher's definition of success. This is considered in terms of eight elements: conscientiousness and integrity, decisiveness, emotional resilience, influence, interpersonal sensitivity, motivation and self-awareness. The teacher explains:

Now if we get people to define how they perform, I think […] these eight [elements] [are] what we really want to have in our own definitions of success. Not ten out of ten because I can write and read and have a good memory.

Student nominations and peer voting for merits or commendations

Another essential element of this teacher's approach is to ask the students to find their own criteria for success and to transfer the responsibility to them for rewarding each others' good work.

They nominate each other for merits or commendations ... we've got various systems that they've come up with; we just move these systems around.

To do this they have to make their criteria explicit under three headings.

We ask ourselves, 'What do you mean by 'volunteering'? What do you mean by 'behaviour'? What do you mean by 'presentation of a book'?

The teacher may then ask for nominations – students who have been successful in meeting the criteria they have explored. Suppose, as happened, Addison and Aaron are nominated for 'good behaviour'. Students then vote for each person nominated. The teacher then asks:

Who would like to vote for Addison because his behaviour has been good enough to get a merit this half term – twenty people – and for Aaron, sixteen, and for Craig, six for Craig. After those have been counted – and of course it's not me who does all this, it's the LSA or the students who write all these down. We will then go to Addison and say, 'Addison, twenty people have suggested that you deserve a merit for this half term's 'behaviour' or 'volunteering' or whatever. What about you, Addison? Do you think you deserve one?' and, as you can see, some people have even got fourteen people who have voted for them and they've declined it. So why is that? Why will they decline this? Because they know, in their heart of hearts that they want to try a bit harder. We've got to turn it round, we've got to ask people to be honest because if you're not, then you can't measure yourself and then target where you want to be in the future. [...] Honesty has to come first [after] the nominations, and then of course it's communal approbation, isn't it? And hopefully that snowball will be a positive snowball rather than a put-down.

Deciding on the three headings, behaviour, volunteering and presentation

The ones chosen in one class were 'behaviour', 'volunteering' and 'presentation of book' but it could be anything. It's up to the class to go with however many they want. Three is a good number because otherwise it gets too long, [and] takes too long to do. I like that system because it's students being involved.

Awarding merits under each heading

The students have decided that if you have five ones – eins – in a row, you get a merit. If you have ten you have two merits. If you have fifteen you get three merits and a commendation. There are now children who are on 32 ones in a row, 32 excellent lessons in a row. There are some dodgy children here, in the groups that I work with and they feel good about that – [and get] as you have just heard, a round of applause. That was Helen [a trainee teacher working in the open space outside]. That's a dodgy class outside. How do we get [...] other people who get parachuted in from outside – a trainee teacher or a qualified teacher – to [...] employ these strategies? – Not all of them do because it's hard. But [practices] that they feel comfortable with [they] make [...] their own. This is not a prescription, it's a suggestion, [...] a framework.

Progress sheets and student self-evaluations

This was work in progress.

We are now working on the whole-school progress sheets at the end of a half-term, two terms, whatever, and [when] reports go out. Instead of us writing one to fives or A to Bs with 'satisfactory' in the middle – I want to get rid of that –we use the one, two, three, four system so that all the reports go out with 'excellent' 'good', 'can improve a little bit' 'must improve an awful lot'. [...] We have got rid of the sitting on the fence '3C – adequate/satisfactory'; horrible, isn't it? If anyone told my daughter [she was] 'adequate/satisfactory' I'd be up to the school saying, 'What does that mean?' and of course no student understands it anyway because they think 'satisfactory' means something actually positive. We [must] examine our words for success; if the students are confused, mums and dads at home are confused. [...] If we use five [as the lowest grade] students are going with poor, poor, poor labelled on their forehead. What's the message there? Can't we be positive in our language [as] the poster said. If we're asking the students to be positive, we've got to examine our own practice.

Half-year meetings which address the question 'Why are we here?'

So back to that question 'Why are we here?' and this is a crux. Do we really give the silent majority the chance to have a voice? And this is where we're at – why are we here? How about giving this silent majority a chance to have a voice. [...] These half-year meetings, as I've explained with the half-year groups – a hundred doing French, a hundred people doing German in each year. These half-year meetings hopefully won't just be me doing a Billy Graham in front of everyone ... eventually it will be the students running the meetings themselves. Why are we here? What do we want out of this? And we link [the question] with all the things that we've said so far [about] giving the silent majority a voice. A wonderful quote [...]; a supply teacher was taking a Year 7 last year, and said [to me] 'Do you know, some of the girls came up and said, 'Miss, that's the first time a man's ever listened to us'. That actually stuck, quite profoundly.

Keeping video recordings of pupils' comments in the half-yearly 'why are we here' meetings

We've got, as you know, hundreds of hours of students on video-tape because that's their record of achievement; three hours of video tape from Year 7 to Year 11. [...] We have to ask permission from them for another year group to see them. You need permission, don't you, before using the quotes. We've started writing down Year 7 quotes from these meetings. As you can see, we've got quite a few. 'Why are you here?', 'Because I want to learn some German'; 'I'm here not only to learn German but to learn how to communicate'; 'To learn'; 'Because it's the law'; Now that's the one you want, 'because it's the law' – why you're here. You can really work with that one. 'So you never break the law do you, Chris?' Everyone laughs. 'I know you break the law, Chris. Yeah, I think I saw you break the law. I saw you in your mum's car going at 71 miles an hour down the road, going down the motorway. Oh, I break the law as well Chris, don't worry. I think we all break the law, don't we? So it's not the law, is it Chris? There must be some other reason you come here.' 'Yes, my mum, Sir' 'Oh, so you do everything your mum says, do you Chris?' Everyone laughs because Chris doesn't. 'So it's not the law, it's not your mum, Chris, why do you come here?' 'To see my mates, Sir' 'Right Chris, so if you want to come and see your mates, wouldn't it be nice to sort of enjoy it while you're here.' And then we go on. We want 'because it's the law' and we turn it around, etc. Now all these notes – Year 11, Year 10, Year 8, Year 9, we've put onto [disk]. [...] We've put it onto disk so we can use it. (...) We've got a data projector in languages and we use it a lot [...] so we'll hopefully be able to find [quotes] quickly.

Exploring with classes what 'care', 'respect' mean, and 'why are we here?'

If we've decided that 'care' or 'respect' is something we're going to look at, [we talk about] what is 'care', what it means. Where does the word [...] come from. A [child in] Year 7 – [a fortnight after I had arrived here last year] – said 'care is when you look after something and don't ruin it. Respect is not leading people out.' [This] is a silent majority having a chance to speak. It's not the boisterous boys. [...] Suddenly little girls put their hands up and say, 'If you show people respect, you earn respect.' Everyone has the right to speak their minds and not be laughed at'. This is the Year 7s, two weeks into [me] being here. Then [there was] the Year 7 German group, [when answering the question why are we here]. Some of these, like Chris, said 'because it's the law'.

'How many people do you think are forced to come to school then, Chris?'. '500 out of 1,040?'.

'50%, Sir.'

'Oh, a mathematical mind. 500. Where does that come from?'

[...] They think 500 people are forced to come to school out of 1,040 and then someone else will say zero 'because nobody can make you do anything'. Vincent said this. Back to the premise, we can't teach anyone anything unless they want to learn. We can't force them. [...] How do we turn the National Curriculum into something they want to do? Instead of just ramming it down throats we're going to say, 'There are some teachers around here. Why are they here?' There are some lovely answers. We refresh our memory with this using the data projector. Vincent's wonderful answer. Why are the adults here?' 'To teach, to get a job?' And we turn it around.

*'Is it a good wage packet?' Turn it around 'Actually we don't want to teach you anything. We (teachers), we want to **learn**. We are interested in you, how you learn – kinaesthetic, auditory – we want to learn how Johnny works, we want to learn how Sarah works compared to Johnny and we want you to teach each other. [...] Everyone agreed to these three principles and we go back to those ones. And then we discuss what are the most important skills for learning as we said, eye contact. And the lovely one about the Chinese word 'to listen.' Apparently 'to listen' in Chinese encompasses listening with the ears but also with your eyes. You listen with your eyes – eye-contact obviously. But most importantly you listen with your heart. If you heart's not in it ... So we try and get that across and we say, 'look, we're not going to go on unless a hundred faces are looking this way. But also, just put your hand up if your heart's in it.' [...] A bit dodgy! But after a few times of talking it through people understand. Even Year 7s. In fact Year 7s understand it beautifully. It's the Year 9s you have to try and catch. [...] Going through the question again we say, 'You don't come into the languages area if you do not want to be part of this invitation. Can we get this in our heads, please? We are not going to stop other people's learning are we? Back to you. What do you want out of this?'*

Dealing with pupils calling out in class

Pupils calling out is a phenomenon which happens in every year group. On the database there is evidence that this was reported in meetings with Year 7, 9 and 11. The teacher's way of dealing with this is to involve pupils in trying to work out the causes.

Gemma, Stuart and Jamie have decided to observe in future what happens to stop lessons and they're going to report back to the next meeting. [This discussion] will last the entire lesson – an hour. But we can have half-hour sessions if we feel that a group is going a bit askew. The meetings are positive and negative, [...] [If they are] negative at first [...] you need to get them back into thinking positively. If we need to have three groups remind the one, [...] why we're here, then we do that. [...] Let's use the students as a resource, [as well as] overhead project, video camera. These are the resources that we need to use.

Students' taking responsibility for their own learning

We must get our children to understand that it's their choice in what they are doing and they are the ones in control; we've got to give them the opportunity to be in control and the language to do it. We have to encourage errors and discourage mistakes. What is the difference between an error and a mistake? You can only make a mistake if you fail to acknowledge your error.

A focus on homework

10

A history of 'the homework challenge' by Moira Edmunds, Support Teacher, Modern Languages, Angus Council, Scotland

---

Diary of a homework experiment

August

Problems

a S4 (15 year-olds): only one pupil got a Grade 1 in Credit Writing as the department records show.

b S5 (16 year-olds): my class last year had no idea how to assume responsibility for their own research in their studies of literature/criticism of texts/correcting their own errors.

c I needed to invent interesting tasks for Credit Writing in S4 and build-up to writing an essay in younger classes.

Tentative solution

I decided to make some changes to more independence in S3 (14 year-olds) so that I would never have another S5 so reluctant to do things for themselves. I presented my homework choice experiment to the pupils in S3 as:

- a way of practising writing;

- a way of producing exercises and work and word displays for others, especially younger pupils in S1, S2;

- a way of encouraging and celebrating their own creativity, choice, personal research and achievement;

- a different approach to necessary homework;

- they would be in charge, working in groups to help administer the choice and collection of homework.

November

S3 homework: First steps

I issued:

1 A **jotter** per group for the recording of homework intentions.

2 A **folder** for each group to put homework in on a Tuesday morning (bought folders).

3 Bought **pad** (no paper in department) for homework. Supplied an audio tape for each group (my own tapes).

4   Appointed **group leader** per group – class new to me – selection had no particular basis for making choice.

5   Moved two boys on their own who don't participate much into two separate groups for homework purposes making:

Group 1	5	Group 4	5	
Group 2	4	Group 5	4	= class of 26
Group 3	4	Group 6	4	

Week 1: Start of November

Introduction to S3 homework – explained in English

I tell the class that they are to do one piece of written homework per week which will be selected on a Tuesday morning which is the first day of the week they have French. They will then have one week in which to do the piece.

I tell them that they will each choose a piece from a typed sheet of choices (see *'Le défi-devoirs'*, pages 60–62). I told them the English version would help them explain to their parents what they had picked (see pages 62–64).

They then have to record their homework selection by getting the Group Leader to write in the jotter under the appropriate date.

Each pupil at the top of his homework sheet should record in French his name, where he is doing the homework, the time at which he starts and the state of the weather and the date. This gets rid of the blank page angst.

I tell them that when I correct their work they will get a number of marks for Effort, Presentation and the use of French. I then ask them, if they were teachers, what would please them under these headings and make them want to allocate good marks.

When I take the box file home with their group folders inside I decide to stick on the outside of each folder a record of their marks for each of the items – Effort, Presentation and French together with spaces for the Date and Comment. These were ranged beside the names of each pupil in the group and the group number. My marks and comments were handwritten onto prepared sheets with the names and the information below.

le 2 février	Effort	Présentation	Français	Commentaire	Total
Blair	10	10	9	Great work! You could make a book of these.	29
Richard	10	10	10	Good use of colour adjectives. Well done! You can display immediately.	30
Mathew	10	10	10	Amazing work! Can I be your manager? Put it on the wall in the corridor under 'Groupe 2'	30
Ryan	10	9	10	Good work, Ryan!	29

Week 2: At the weekend

On looking at their work I am impressed by the lengths some have gone to present their work neatly and some have added artwork even when the topic did not require it – a wordsearch on women's jewellery had beautifully drawn illustrations. A menu had fruit and vegetables as decoration.

Where a drawing formed an integral part of the choice as in 'Draw a picture of a person/object and describe it' the ideas were wonderful. One boy drew a washing machine with a cat inside it and the carefully labelled machine indicated in French what was happening to the cat.

I looked at the errors and knew I couldn't ruin the pages with red ink. I would like to be able to record my method in correcting but it varied. My main pre-occupation was to promote confidence and increase motivation. They were all choosing different pieces of work and I did not need to have anything like a marking scheme so I will record some of the things I did when marking and then illustrate the consequences.

Week 2: Homework arrives – marking

I took the homework pieces home at the weekend.

I treated the pieces of work differently according to what I knew of the pupil and how brave (or foolhardy) they had been in selecting their piece.

For example – copy-writing.

1   A boy X had chosen to write numbers (learn and write out). This looked like a soft option and was chosen by three boys. All the pieces contained mistakes. I wrote on X's piece of work that he had to find out where the numerals were listed in his textbook and re-copy the numerals accurately. I expressed horror that they might have learned such mistakes (I was in no doubt that they had learned little from the whole exercise). When the class arrived on the following Tuesday I told all the boys that they were going to work together to produce an important worksheet/grammar sheet for the class on numbers. The worksheet was to contain a reference to the pages in the textbook where accurate numerals could be found. For some I'm sure this was going to be the first time the books had been opened. They were also to rewrite their piece for display.

2   I put a small dot to indicate a spelling error in the labelling on the feline washing machine, and indicated with arrows any word order problems. In class I suggested to the pupil that with the help of some paper and glue he could rewrite his description to make it completely accurate and all he needed was a dictionary after we had discussed the word-order errors. I told him the piece of work would then go straight on the wall as it was so 'great'.

3   To someone who had written a postcard (drawing a stamp and franking marks and sticking on a magazine picture of the holiday destination on the reverse side), I suggested that a bit of correction fluid would sort out a couple of minor errors. I then asked her in the comment section if she would be good enough to make up three questions in English on her postcard's contents so that it could be used as comprehension for another pupil. This could be her homework for next time although she said later she was going to do a menu the next time so she would do the comprehension questions as a piece of work to help me!

Week 3: Self-correcting – following on the marking strategy

For those who had written a menu I did different things for different people.

•   Anyone showing signs of not having researched the work and putting down errors in categories (like making up French words for 'first course') were asked to research a real menu from some I'd brought back from the canteen of a school in France and amend their copies.

- Anyone doing a beautiful, accurate menu was asked to suggest a guided role-play situation in English at the bottom of a separate sheet (I then had to buy paper clips) on which the menu would feature as an essential prop.

- Anyone with mistakes in spelling found red dots and the directive in the comment box to get a dictionary out and/or check any food lists in their textbooks – vocabulary notebooks were not consulted as they didn't always copy accurately into these in the first place.

- Ultimately all the menu writers were asked to make up a role-play exercise using their menu as the essential prop once the corrected version had been produced for use by younger pupils.

More ideas to extend homework pieces

1   Make up a gap-filling exercise from a piece of work. Supply words as solution.

2   Cloze – some of letters missing – words may be provided as solution.

3   Jumble words of several sentences for rearranging and/or linking. Jumbled halves of sentences for putting together.

4   Rearrange sentences to reproduce text.

5   Sentence-building from given elements – in order to write a note for an errand.

Peux-tu aller	à la boulangerie à la crémerie à l'épicerie à la fruiterie	m'acheter	un kilo un paquet six tranches	de beurre? de pain? de jambon? des œufs?

Pupils then began to suggest writing tasks themselves and the list of choices started to grow:

1   Asking and answering questions about themselves – add to homework questions.

2   Write out what you did at the weekend (if it is newsworthy).

3   Describe something you saw – film, TV programme.

4   Leave a note for someone.

5   Leave a note of a phone call.

6   Shopping list.

7   Leave a note to say why you are out.

8   Be a private detective and write about someone's activities you observed. In the same role, write out what they bought.

9   Write a pamphlet.

Other possible writing tasks:

- Expansion, extension or redrafting of given stories or incidents.

- Devising different endings.

- Adding on events and writing them down from the point of view of different participants.

- Make lists of what they know already.

- Make notes of language they find interesting.

- Describe your reaction to a picture.

(For more ideas, see Pathfinder 10: *Being creative* (Jones 1992)).

Week 3: Self-correcting and follow-up

I used the whole period on Week 3 to help pupils see how they could either locate resources to check their work or get in touch with others (by means of a chart on the board showing those who'd made the same errors).

Adjectives	Present tense
Andrew Paul	James

I told them how useful it would be to go on and produce a helpsheet for others in the class who might have problems.

I encouraged them to develop the original piece of work for use with other younger classes or for pupils in another group of their own class.

I also asked permission of two boys to photocopy their wordsearches for use with S2 the next day to leave as 'extra' for those who finished the set work while I was out of school the following day on a visit to the hospital. They were very flattered.

Pupil input improves
Two boys came up and asked me if they could write a French version of an English song since this was not on the list. I agreed and they fell about like gleeful conspirators. The homework was becoming even more varied and the class were obviously enjoying control over the selection.

Week 4

The two conspirators appeared with the words of 'Postman Pat' in French and a recording with great musical backing of them singing it. It was super. We had a chat about the black and white cat which was going to have to become a 'cat black and white'. Andrew therefore learnt about the position of adjectives, Jack learnt about plural verb endings and it was back to the drawing board.

Week 5

I offered to type up the words on the computer. The class members got a copy of the words and we sang along to the new version of the song 'Facteur Pat'. We were having a lot of fun with the homework and the standard was getting higher.

Week 6: Pupil output doubles

Winter holiday then snow disruption.

One of the boys in the class produced two foolscap pages of script for a scene in a dress shop. I suggested he get his group to learn the parts and we would video-tape the result.

Week 7

I added a list of new choices to the original sheet including the song option and underlined the importance of writing Name/Date/Weather/Time/Place on their work. I sometimes have trouble allocating marks to an unknown author.

Snow suspends project for a week.

Summary

Where to now and some theory

- I am looking forward to having a computer in class so that pupils can redraft work.

- The challenge of choosing, adapting and discussing ideas encourages creativity even though choices are directed.

- There is a need for action from them:

  – to prepare work for others;

  – to display work done by your group/yourself;

  – to photocopy work for use with other classes;

  – to test out a piece of work or to check feedback..

- There is a dominant idea – work has to be accurate.

- I always stress in class that the most sophisticated skill is to be able to correct one's own mistakes, to replace mistakes in written work with corrected versions as well as to **say** on a spoken piece *Pardon, je voulais dire plutôt* …

Suggested improvements: homework choices

- For those who choose to learn and write out something there could be a stage in class where another pupil will check selected words which the person is supposed to have learned.

- On a chosen topic they might have three minutes to write down as many of their words with English equivalents as they can. Other pupils then mark them by looking in the textbook to check. In the process they learn a few more words they hadn't chosen for themselves. The teacher should look briefly at the test papers to see the range of words chosen.

- Be prepared to negotiate a choice which brings in the pupil's interests and give the pupil a chance to express his personality through his work in modern languages.

Disadvantages

1   It is time-consuming to set up but will run itself if you get it right. You have to have a Homework leader and a stand-in should that person be absent.

2   It takes much longer to mark work without a marking scheme.

3   Once you get going there is no going back, the pupils will be caught up in making their choices and doing their thing and you might be needing a week off. So when the timetable says exam marking tell the pupils that the project is temporarily suspended.

4   You need a lot of display areas; consider washing lines across the room if the security system can cope with billowing homework.

5   Perhaps you will not have handed back their work and discussed it before they have to make a further choice so you may want to do the handing back a day in advance of the choosing day. In this way if the pupils are to be doing work as an extension of previous work they are forewarned. You may decide to let them choose on week 1, you hand back on week 2, doing then, on week 2, corrections and display in an allocated time slot. They choose again on week 3, picking up necessary materials and resources. This would allow time for research, correction and display and would reduce the pressure of marking by making it into more of an ongoing project than a weekly commitment.

Advantages

1   Parents will tell you that their child loves doing French homework and is already working on something not due for another fortnight.

2   Accuracy and autonomy will be more evident as pupils learn how to achieve it.

3   You will, as I did, be able to send off your pupils' homework to the likes of PGCE students at Cambridge University via their tutor Barry Jones. Each future language teacher adopted a pupil and wrote simple letters of encouragement and praise in French and in English, to the participants of the Homework challenge in Arbroath (see below). Suddenly the pupils had an unexpected Cambridge connection.

Faculty of Education
Head of Faculty: Tim Everton MA MSc

 **UNIVERSITY OF CAMBRIDGE**

Lundi 27 avril

 Chère Susan,

Salut ! Je m'appelle Gaëlle et je suis française. J'aime beaucoup ton travail. C'est SUPER ! Ton 'Livre d'enfants' est très intéressant et amusant, et ta carte de Pâques est très jolie !
Tu habites à Arbroath ? J'habite à Cambridge. J'aime beaucoup le sport : la natation, le volley-ball, le basket-ball ... et j'adore les chats .
Ton français est FANTASTIQUE !

À Bientôt.

G

Homerton Site, Hills Road, Cambridge CB2 2PH
Telephone: 01223 507222   Fax: 01223 507140   Internet: http://www.educ.cam.ac.uk/

Homework challenge (French version): Sheets for pupils

Moira Edmunds, Support Teacher: Modern Languages, Angus Council, Scotland

Le défi-devoirs

Choisis quelque chose de la liste suivante et copie le numéro et les instructions dans ton carnet de devoirs. N'oublie pas ton NOM et la DATE.

1 Je vais trouver une image et mettre des étiquettes dessus.

2 Je vais écrire une bande dessinée avec des paroles en français dans des bulles.

3 Je vais faire une carte (d'anniversaire, de la St Valentin, de Pâques, de Noël).

4 Je vais écrire des dates importantes (les anniversaires de ma famille ou les jours fériés).

5 Je vais écrire une lettre (à un ami, au Père Noël, à mon correspondant).

6 Je vais trouver une photo de ma maison et en faire une description.

7 Je vais écrire une liste de pays francophones.

8 Je vais parler des sports que j'aime et pourquoi je les aime. Je vais aussi parler de ceux que je n'aime pas.

9 Je vais composer une liste d'adjectifs avec des illustrations.

10 Je vais composer un livre d'enfants sur l'alphabet français ou sur un animal.

11 Je vais dessiner une famille avec une description de chaque membre de la famille.

12 Je vais écrire un dialogue.

13 Je vais interviewer une personne importante ou un autre adulte puis en faire un rapport.

14 Je vais écrire un article pour un journal ou un magazine.

15 Je vais découper un article d'un magazine anglais et en faire un résumé en français.

16 Je vais composer un 'mots mêlés' pour un autre élève. Je ne vais pas oublier de faire une copie de la solution sur une autre feuille.

17 Je vais trouver une photo de moi et en faire une description.

18 Je vais dessiner ou trouver des images sur des chiens différents et faire une description de chacun. Je peux choisir des chats aussi ou d'autres animaux.

19 Je vais trouver un dépliant sur ma ville natale at écrire un peu à son sujet en français.

20 Je vais faire un dépliant destiné aux touristes français qui viennent en Ecosse.

21 Je vais faire un arbre généalogique.

22 Je vais faire un document sonore sur cassette, soit à la maison soit au collège au club de devoirs.

23 Je vais écrire une description de mon collège ou de mes professeurs.

24 Je vais faire une description des animaux domestiques de la classe ou préparer un sondage.

25 Je vais faire un sondage et puis en mettre les résultats au mur.

26 Je vais écrire un verbe et en faire une chanson ou des illustrations.

27 Je vais composer une chanson en français ou traduire une chanson anglaise en français. Je vais l'enregistrer après.

28 Je vais raconter une blague en français.

29 Je vais composer un formulaire à remplir.

30 Je vais décrire mon petit ami idéal (ma petite amie pour les garçons).

31 Je vais lire un livre de *Bibliobus* à haute voix et l'enregistrer.

32 Je vais lire un livre de *Bibliobus* et écrire mon opinion sur l'histoire, les illustrations et les personnages.

33 Je vais composer un poème en français.

34 Je vais faire un calendrier illustré.

35 Je vais faire un rapport sur la météo à la mode de la présentatrice à la télé.

36 Je vais enregistrer une chanson française.

37 Je vais faire un poster de quelqu'un recherché par la police.

38 Je vais envoyer un fax en français.

39 Je vais préparer quelque chose sur mon ordinateur en français.

40 Je vais faire autre chose après en avoir parlé au professeur.

Extras

41 Je vais enregistrer un programme pour la radio.

42 Je vais faire des mots croisés avec des questions en anglais et des solutions en français arrangées horizontalement, verticalement et diagonalement.

43 Je vais faire une description d'un professeur ou de quelqu'un de célèbre. Je vais l'appeler peut-être 'Qui est-ce?'

44 Je vais m'asseoir près d'une fenêtre et faire une description de ce que je vois. Je peux faire une scène imaginaire .

45 Je vais monter une petite pièce française.

46 Je vais écrire une petite histoire en français.

47 Je vais dessiner des publicités.

48 Je vais faire une carte du monde avec ses pays.

49 Je vais faire une description de mon ancienne école primaire.

50 Je vais composer mon menu idéal.

51 Je vais faire un puzzle sur carton. N'oublie pas la solution.

52 Je vais créer un jeu de société.

53 Je vais décrire des moyens de transport différents.

54 Je vais classer des mots en catégories ou par thèmes comme les formes ou les couleurs.

55 Je vais raconter l'histoire de ma routine quotidienne.

56 Je vais raconter ce que je vais faire pour les vacances.

57 Je vais faire un petit journal ou un magazine (une page pour commencer).

58 Je vais faire des prévisions astrologiques.

59 Je vais faire des légendes en français et les coller sur mon album d'animaux domestiques et puis le montrer au professeur.

60 Je vais faire un plan de ma ville ou de mon village.

61 Je vais illustrer les planètes et le système solaire.

62 Je vais créer un concours.

63 Je vais raconter l'histoire d'une journée au collège.

64 Je vais faire une liste de Français célèbres.

65 Je vais copier une page du dictionnaire ou choisir un morceau intéressant.

66 Je vais écrire quelque chose sur les emplois.

Section sur le football

67 Je vais décrire un joueur de foot.

68 Je vais dessiner tous les drapeaux de la Coupe du Monde.

69 Je vais dessiner un stade de foot.

70 Je vais inventer des maillots de foot.

71 Je vais inventer tout l'équipement d'une équipe de football.

72 Je vais décrire mon équipe de rêve.

73 Je vais écrire une conversation imaginaire entre un joueur de foot et moi.

Homework challenge (English version): Sheets for parents

Moira Edmunds, Support Teacher Modern Languages, Angus Council, Scotland

Choose something from the following list and copy the number and the instructions into your homework jotter. Do not forget your NAME and the DATE.

1 I am going to find a picture and put labels on it.

2 I am going to do a cartoon with words in French in speech bubbles.

3 I am going to make a card (birthday, St Valentine's, Easter, Christmas).

4 I am going to write down some important dates (family birthdays or holidays).

5 I am going to write a letter (to a friend, to Santa, to my penpal).

6 I am going to find a picture of my house and describe it.

7 I am going to write a list of French-speaking countries.

8 I am going to speak about sports I like and why I like them. I am also going to talk about those I don't like.

9 I am going to write a list of adjectives with illustrations.

10 I am going to make a children's book on the alphabet or on an animal.

11 I am going to draw a family with a description of each member.

12 I am going to write a dialogue of a conversation.

13 I am going to interview an important person or another adult and then make a report on the conversation.

14 I am going to write an article for a newspaper or magazine.

15 I am going to cut out an article from an English magazine and do a summary of it in French.

16 I am going to make up a wordsearch for another pupil. I am not going to forget to make a copy of the solution.

17 I am going to find a photo of myself and do a description of it.

18 I am going to draw or find pictures of different dogs and do a description of each one. I can choose cats also or different animals.

19 I am going to find a brochure on my home town and write a little about it.

20 I am going to do a brochure for French tourists coming to Scotland.

21 I am going to do a family tree.

22 I am going to do a tape either at home or at school in the homework club.

23 I am going to write a description of my school or teachers.

24 I am going to write a description of the pets we have in our class or do a survey.

25 I am going to do a survey and put the results on the wall.

26 I am going to write down a verb and make up a song about it or illustrate it.

27 I am going to compose a song in French or translate an English song into French. I am going to record it afterwards.

28 I am going to tell a joke in French.

29 I am going to make up a form for filling in.

30 I am going to describe my ideal boyfriend (girlfriend for boys).

31 I am going to read a *Bibliobus* book aloud and record it.

32 I am going to read a *Bibliobus* book and write my opinion on the story, the illustrations and the characters.

33 I am going to compose a poem in French.

34 I am going to do an illustrated calendar.

35 I am going to do a weather report like the presenter on the television.

36 I am going to record a French song.

37 I am going to do a police 'Wanted' poster.

38 I am going to send a fax in French.

39 I am going to prepare something on my computer in French.

40 I am going to do some other things worked out after speaking to the teacher.

Extras

41 I am going to tape a radio show.

42 I am going to do a crossword with English questions and French solutions arranged horizontally and vertically.

43 I am going to do a description of a teacher or someone well known. I might call it 'Who is this?'

44 I am going to sit at a window and describe what I see. I could describe an imaginary scenario.

45 I am going to do a small French play.

46 I am going to write a short story in French.

47 I am going to design some advertisements.

48 I am going to do a map of the world and its countries.

49 I am going to do a description of my old primary school.

50 I am going to compose my ideal menu.

51 I am going to make a jigsaw of French words and pictures on cardboard. Don't forget to include the answers.

52 I am going to make a board game.

53 I am going to describe different kinds of transport.

54 I am going to put some words I know into categories like shapes or colours.

55 I am going to do my daily routine.

56 I am going to say what I am going to do during the holidays.

57 I am going to make a little French newspaper or magazine, a single page to start off.

58 I am going to make up horoscopes.

59 I am going to write some French onto 'Post-its' and stick them on my Pet album to show the teacher.

60 I am going to do a map of my town.

61 I am going to illustrate the planets and solar system.

62 I am going to design a competition.

63 I am going to outline the story of a school day.

64 I am going to write a list of famous French people.

65 I am going to copy a dictionary page or copy an interesting bit from one.

66 I am going to write about jobs.

Football section

67 I am going to describe a footballer.

68 I am going to draw and label all the flags from the World Cup.

69 I am going to draw and label a football stadium.

70 I am going to invent some football strips.

71 I am going to design my own football kit.

72 I am going to describe my dream team.

73 I am going to write an imaginary conversation between a footballer and myself.

At the end of the homework challenge, pupils were awarded this certificate to show the teacher's recognition of their achievement.

Certificat

Nom, prénom ....

Classe ....

has taken part in the Homework Challenge known in French as 'le Défi-Devoirs' and gained

_____ marks out of _____ marks

between   and

The work produced has been marked for effort, presentation and accurate French.

Signature .... Date ....

Signature du professeur .... Date ....

Conclusion

The purpose of both the initial study and the follow-up school-based projects was to explore ways to help boys in particular to think about and improve their language learning. In the three years of the study's existence and throughout many discussions with teachers it has become clear that, although the focus was purportedly on boys, many projects have been more about questioning what we – and the pupils – do in our modern foreign language classrooms. Sometimes teachers' beliefs have been confirmed, sometimes they have been challenged. At the very least the projects have convincingly demonstrated the complexity of foreign language teaching and learning in school. This has frequently been revealed as a web of factors some of which may influence why some boys respond enthusiastically to what teachers do in class and others where the response is more reluctant. Cause and effect are not always clear. However, by consistently reviewing classroom practice and by speaking to pupils on a one-to-one basis, changes of attitude can result and, as a consequence, working methods change. What is also quite remarkable is that, more often than not, learners know precisely what they need to do to improve. It is clear that what we, as teachers, can do more of is to explore with them how they work best, what, from a list of options, they would choose to help themselves get better, in brief what they think. It is then up to us to provide opportunities for their thoughts, mediated through our discussions with them, to be translated into action with perhaps less focus on teachers' teaching and more on learners' learning. This book may help focus discussion within MFL departments and provide a range of activities for teachers and learners to share, explore and evaluate together. For discussion key issues can be summarised as:

Audience Choice Consistency Purpose Fun Boys in charge ICT Responsibility MFL as means to something Promoting MFL; high status Interactive explanations & models Performing to others Rewards Recap possibilities

Acknowledgements

Many teachers attended initial meetings which had been arranged to introduce the theme of improving boys' performance in MFL. Those whom I would like to thank are the participants who returned for the regional follow-up sessions and those who reported what they had achieved between the two, three or four dates. These were also teachers who sent in reports of activities in which they had been involved who were not always able to attend meetings, and a number of Post Graduate Certificate of Education (PGCE) students in Bristol university and on the Key Stage 2/3 course in the Faculty of Education, Cambridge University, who contributed ideas for practice which they had explored in the classroom. It is to all these teachers and student-teachers as well as to those who helped in the organisation of or who contributed to meetings that my sincerest thanks are due. Without their efforts, ideas and commitment this book would not have been possible.

Bristol and Avon group

Ben Allen, Christine Balandier-Brown, Allison Bolster, Lois Bradley, Liz Eastham, Mark Etherington, Mélanie Guillot, Elisabeth Lazarus, Fekaj Sheribon, Anne Steel, Sarah Thomas, Gaynor Vaughan.

Essex group

Sophie Childs, Nick Gibbs, Fiona Giles, Emma Kilburn, Renate Lotz, Gee Mackie, Richard Mason, Peter Reader, Avril Reynolds, Kay Sharpe, D. Stokes, Sylvie Vahé, Manuela Ward, Chris Wright.

Leicestershire group

Jill Cartmel, Anne Fanthorpe, Pam Hazewindt, Jill Jennison, Jacqueline Newcombe, Silja Pike, Anne Roberts, Gill West, Katharine Wright.

North East Comenius group; meeting in Sunderland

Diane Bolingbroke, Phil Drabble, Paul Gaffney, Jo Hardy, Sue Hyland, Tom Kingston, Bill Lacey, Lyn Marsay, Marie Mills, Karen Roberts, Florence Touvy, Margaret Turner, Chris Williams.

North West Comenius group; meeting in Lancaster and Carlisle

Judy Carruthers, Frances Dent, Alison Gilvey, Nathalie Hannan, Jane Heggedus, John Page, Rhona Rutter, Julia Seggie, Clive Sheldon, Lisa Stephenson, Mike Travers.

Somerset group

Christelle Arzur, Bridget Caddy, Dominique Chadwick, Eva Heim-Butler, Eve Gilbert, Lesley Hooper, Valerie McIntyre, Barbara Myerson, Jonathan Peace, Jenny Peppard, Alan Pringle, Shirley Randall, Jane Sanders, Annie Singer, Joanne Stephens, Lorna Weeks.

Wales: Bangor group

Sian Beidas, Sue Entwistle, Keith Marshall, Anthea Payne, Ann Vaughan.

Wales: Cardiff group

Caroline Crabb, Karen Critchley, Claire Davies, Caroline Douglas Jones, Kelly Gifford, Frédérique Horton, Laura Hurn, Carol Izri, Ceri James, Holger Kroll, Alison Lang, Rebecca Maggs, Pamela Marsh, Stephan Morris, Neil Owen, Vani Paterianaki, Kelly Rome.

Thanks are also due to Simon Green, CILT, for setting up a meeting in Leeds, Dr Jo Carr from the Faculty of Education, Queensland University of Technology, Australia, for sharing her work on Boys' Performance in MFL in Australia, Amélie Année for her engaging and astonishing Teach a Friend a Language (TAFAL) project based at Woodbridge High School and Language College, Woodford Green, Essex, which won a European Award for Languages, Dirk Pereira, Ernulf Community College, St Neots, Cambridgeshire, for his time, captivating classroom practice and clear, all-embracing school policy which was so impressive to see in operation, and Moira Edmunds, Support Teacher: Modern Languages, Angus Council, Scotland, for her inspirational work on homework and homework policies, to Emma Rees and Anna Samuels for their editorial input. Finally my thanks are most due to my wife, Gwenneth for her support, ideas and encouragement.

References

DfES (2005) *The languages ladder – steps to success*. DfES.

Goleman, D. (1996) *Emotional intelligence: why it can matter more than IQ*. Bloomsbury

Jones, B. (1992) Pathfinder 10: *Being creative*. CILT, the National Centre for Languages.

Jones, B., and Jones, G. et al (2001) *Boys' performance in Modern Foreign Languages: Listening to learners*. CILT.

Jones, B. and Swarbrick, A. (2004) New Pathfinder 4: *It makes you think: Creating engagement, offering challenges*. CILT, the National Centre for Languages.

Robson, M. and McGuiness, J. (ed) (1999) 'Symposium: guidance and counselling in schools', *British Journal of Guidance and Counselling*, Volume 27, Number 1, February 1999.

Swarbrick, A. (1998) Pathfinder 36: *More reading for pleasure*. CILT.

Further reading

For a general, non-MFL specific treatment of the theme of boys' underachievement recommended are two journal articles, although there are many more:

- Younger, M., Warrington, M. and McLellan, R. (2002) 'The "problem" of "under-achieving boys" Some responses from English secondary schools', *School Leadership and Management*, Vol. 22, No.4: 389–405.

- Clarke, P. (1999) 'Talking with boys to facilitate new thinking about their learning', *Improving schools*, Volume 2, Number 1.

The following are very detailed and comprehensive sources of references for those readers who wish to explore this theme in detail and with reference to MFL:

- Carr, J. and Pauwels, A. (2005) *Real boys don't do languages*. Palgrave Macmillan.

- Sunderland, J. (2000) 'Issues of language and gender in second and foreign language education' (review article) in *Language Teaching*. Cambridge University Press.

Further, selected reading is included in:

- Barton, A. (2003) *Getting the buggers into languages*. Continuum. See the chapter 'Gender and achievement'.

- Pachler, N. and Field, K. (1999) Learning to teach Modern Foreign Languages in the secondary school (1999). Routledge. Included is a simple observation/reflection activity (Chapter 8, p181) on gender differences and pre-emptive/remedial action. Although this ignores many issues which have been explored in this book and elsewhere it may provide a useful beginning, especially for student teachers who by definition are new to MFL classroom practice.

A more substantial contribution is the chapter by Kit Field *'Why are girls better at Modern Foreign Languages than boys?'* (pp130–142) in Field, K. (ed) (2000) *Issues in Modern Foreign Languages Teaching*. Routledge/Falmer.

In Ann Swarbrick's (2002) excellent reader *Teaching Modern Foreign Languages in secondary schools* (published by Routledge/Falmer and the Open University) there are two relevant chapters and bibliographies; firstly one entitled 'Treading a tightrope: Supporting boys to achieve in MFL' by Vee Harris (pp187–202) and secondly, 'Learning styles: The gender effect' by Amanda Barton (pp272–285).

For practical suggestions, see Hartley-Brewer, E. (2000) *Self-esteem for boys: 100 tips*. Vermillion.

boys'
performance
in modern foreign languages

listening to learners

A project carried out
by Homerton College, Cambridge
on behalf of QCA

Barry Jones
Gwenneth Jones

WITH CONTRIBUTIONS FROM

Helen Demetriou
Peter Downes
Jean Rudduck

Boys' performance in Modern Foreign Languages presents research findings and recommendations resulting from a project on boys' under-achievement carried out by Homerton College, Cambridge on behalf of QCA. The findings, based on interviews and focus groups with boys – and some girls – in Years 9 and 11, are presented along with sample evidence – including some hard-hitting quotes. It also includes recommendations from the research team, formulated partly as a response to the problems identified, but drawing also on the boys' positive experiences and suggestions. *Boys' performance in MFL* is essential reading for anyone concerned to understand the reasons behind boys' under-achievement in languages and to support all learners in reaching their full potential.